R. Rubenstein

Connected ❦ Mathematics™

Combinatorics

Teacher's Edition

D1716799

Glenda Lappan
James T. Fey
William M. Fitzgerald
Susan N. Friel
Elizabeth Difanis Phillips

Developed at Michigan State University

DALE SEYMOUR PUBLICATIONS®
MENLO PARK, CALIFORNIA

Connected Mathematics™ was developed at Michigan State University with financial support from the Michigan State University Office of the Provost, Computing and Technology, and the College of Natural Science.

This material is based upon work supported by the National Science Foundation under Grant No. MDR 9150217.

This project was supported, in part,
by the
National Science Foundation
Opinions expressed are those of the authors
and not necessarily those of the Foundation

The Michigan State University authors and administration have agreed that all MSU royalties arising from this publication will be devoted to purposes supported by the Department of Mathematics and the MSU Mathematics Education Enrichment Fund.

This book is published by Dale Seymour Publications®, an imprint of Addison Wesley Longman, Inc.

Dale Seymour Publications
2725 Sand Hill Road
Menlo Park, CA 94025
Customer Service: 800-872-1100

Managing Editor: Catherine Anderson
Project Editor: Stacey Miceli
Book Editor: Mali Apple
ESL Consultant: Nancy Sokol Green
Production/Manufacturing Director: Janet Yearian
Production/Manufacturing Coordinator: Claire Flaherty
Design Manager: John F. Kelly
Photo Editor: Roberta Spieckerman
Design: Don Taka
Composition: London Road Design, Palo Alto, CA
Illustrations: Pauline Phung, Margaret Copeland, Ray Godfrey
Cover: Ray Godfrey

Photo Acknowledgements: 12 © Michael J. Okeniewski/The Image Works; 13 © Ann and Myron Sutton/FPG International; 22 © Geoffrey Apple; 34 © Miro Vintoniv/Stock, Boston; 38 © Nick Dolding/Tony Stone Images

Many of the designations used by manufacturers to distinguish their products are claimed as trademarks. Where those designations appear in this book, and Dale Seymour Publications® was aware of a trademark claim, the designations have been printed in initial caps or all caps.

Cuisenaire is a registered trademark of the Cuisenaire Company of America.

Copyright © 1998 by Michigan State University, Glenda Lappan, James T. Fey, William M. Fitzgerald, Susan N. Friel, and Elizabeth D. Phillips. All rights reserved.

This Book is Printed
on Recycled Paper

Limited reproduction permission: The publisher grants permission to individual teachers who have purchased this book to reproduce the blackline masters as needed for use with their own students. Reproduction for an entire school or school district or for commercial use is prohibited.

Order number 21488
ISBN 1-57232-193-8

2 3 4 5 6 7 8 9 10-ML-01 00 99 98 97

The Connected Mathematics Project Staff

Project Directors

James T. Fey
University of Maryland

William M. Fitzgerald
Michigan State University

Susan N. Friel
University of North Carolina at Chapel Hill

Glenda Lappan
Michigan State University

Elizabeth Difanis Phillips
Michigan State University

Project Manager

Kathy Burgis
Michigan State University

Technical Coordinator

Judith Martus Miller
Michigan State University

Collaborating Teachers/Writers

Mary K. Bouck
Portland, Michigan

Jacqueline Stewart
Okemos, Michigan

Curriculum Development Consultants

David Ben-Chaim
Weizmann Institute

Alex Friedlander
Weizmann Institute

Eleanor Geiger
University of Maryland

Jane Miller
University of Maryland

Jane Mitchell
University of North Carolina at Chapel Hill

Anthony D. Rickard
Alma College

Evaluation Team

Mark Hoover
Michigan State University

Diane V. Lambdin
Indiana University

Sandra K. Wilcox
Michigan State University

Judith S. Zawojewski
National-Louis University

Graduate Assistants

Scott J. Baldridge
Michigan State University

Angie S. Eshelman
Michigan State University

M. Faaiz Gierdien
Michigan State University

Jane M. Keiser
Indiana University

Angela S. Krebs
Michigan State University

James M. Larson
Michigan State University

Ronald Preston
Indiana University

Tat Ming Sze
Michigan State University

Sarah Theule-Lubienski
Michigan State University

Jeffrey J. Wanko
Michigan State University

Field Test Production Team

Katherine Oesterle
Michigan State University

Stacey L. Otto
University of North Carolina at Chapel Hill

Teacher/Assessment Team

Kathy Booth
Waverly, Michigan

Anita Clark
Marshall, Michigan

Julie Faulkner
Traverse City, Michigan

Theodore Gardella
Bloomfield Hills, Michigan

Yvonne Grant
Portland, Michigan

Linda R. Lobue
Vista, California

Suzanne McGrath
Chula Vista, California

Nancy McIntyre
Troy, Michigan

Mary Beth Schmitt
Traverse City, Michigan

Linda Walker
Tallahassee, Florida

Software Developer

Richard Burgis
East Lansing, Michigan

Development Center Directors

Nicholas Branca
San Diego State University

Dianne Briars
Pittsburgh Public Schools

Frances R. Curcio
New York University

Perry Lanier
Michigan State University

J. Michael Shaughnessy
Portland State University

Charles Vonder Embse
Central Michigan University

Field Test Coordinators

Michelle Bohan
Queens, New York

Melanie Branca
San Diego, California

Alecia Devantier
Shepherd, Michigan

Jenny Jorgensen
Flint, Michigan

Sandra Kralovec
Portland, Oregon

Sonia Marsalis
Flint, Michigan

William Schaeffer
Pittsburgh, Pennsylvania

Karma Vince
Toledo, Ohio

Virginia Wolf
Pittsburgh, Pennsylvania

Shirel Yaloz
Queens, New York

Student Assistants

Laura Hammond
David Roche
Courtney Stoner
Jovan Trpovski
Julie Valicenti
Michigan State University

Advisory Board

Joseph Adney
Michigan State University (Emeritus)

Charles Allan
Michigan Department of Education

Mary K. Bouck
Portland Public Schools
Portland, Michigan

C. Stuart Brewster
Palo Alto, California

Anita Clark
Marshall Public Schools
Marshall, Michigan

David Doherty
GMI Engineering and Management Institute
Flint, Michigan

Kay Gilliland
EQUALS
Berkeley, California

David Green
GMI Engineering and Management Institute
Flint, Michigan

Henry Heikkinen
University of Northern Colorado
Greeley, Colorado

Anita Johnston
Jackson Community College
Jackson, Michigan

Elizabeth M. Jones
Lansing School District
Lansing, Michigan

Jim Landwehr
AT&T Bell Laboratories
Murray Hill, New Jersey

Peter Lappan
Michigan State University

Steven Leinwand
Connecticut Department of Education

Nancy McIntyre
Troy Public Schools
Troy, Michigan

Valerie Mills
Ypsilanti Public Schools
Ypsilanti, Michigan

David S. Moore
Purdue University
West Lafayette, Indiana

Ralph Oliva
Texas Instruments
Dallas, Texas

Richard Phillips
Michigan State University

Jacob Plotkin
Michigan State University

Dawn Pysarchik
Michigan State University

Rheta N. Rubenstein
University of Windsor
Windsor, Ontario, Canada

Susan Jo Russell
TERC
Cambridge, Massachusetts

Marjorie Senechal
Smith College
Northampton, Massachusetts

Sharon Senk
Michigan State University

Jacqueline Stewart
Okemos School District
Okemos, Michigan

Uri Treisman
University of Texas
Austin, Texas

Irvin E. Vance
Michigan State University

Linda Walker
Tallahassee Public Schools
Tallahassee, Florida

Gail Weeks
Northville Public Schools
Northville, Michigan

Pilot Teachers

California

National City

Laura Chavez
National City Middle School

Ruth Ann Duncan
National City Middle School

Sonia Nolla
National City Middle School

San Diego

James Ciolli
Los Altos Elementary School

Chula Vista

Agatha Graney
Hilltop Middle School

Suzanne McGrath
Eastlake Elementary School

Toni Miller
Hilltop Middle School

Lakeside

Eva Hollister
Tierra del Sol Middle School

Vista

Linda LoBue
Washington Middle School

Illinois

Evanston

Marlene Robinson
Baker Demonstration School

Michigan

Bloomfield Hills

Roxanne Cleveland
Bloomfield Hills Middle School

Constance Kelly
Bloomfield Hills Middle School

Tim Loula
Bloomfield Hills Middle School

Audrey Marsalese
Bloomfield Hills Middle School

Kara Reid
Bloomfield Hills Middle School

Joann Schultz
Bloomfield Hills Middle School

Flint

Joshua Coty
Holmes Middle School

Brenda Duckett-Jones
Brownell Elementary School

Lisa Earl
Holmes Middle School

Anne Heidel
Holmes Middle School

Chad Meyers
Brownell Elementary School

Greg Mickelson
Holmes Middle School

Rebecca Ray
Holmes Middle School

Patricia Wagner
Holmes Middle School

Greg Williams
Gundry Elementary School

Lansing

Susan Bissonette
Waverly Middle School

Kathy Booth
Waverly East Intermediate School

Carole Campbell
Waverly East Intermediate School

Gary Gillespie
Waverly East Intermediate School

Denise Kehren
Waverly Middle School

Virginia Larson
Waverly East Intermediate School

Kelly Martin
Waverly Middle School

Laurie Metevier
Waverly East Intermediate School

Craig Paksi
Waverly East Intermediate School

Tony Pecoraro
Waverly Middle School

Helene Rewa
Waverly East Intermediate School

Arnold Stiefel
Waverly Middle School

Portland

Bill Carlton
Portland Middle School

Kathy Dole
Portland Middle School

Debby Flate
Portland Middle School

Yvonne Grant
Portland Middle School

Terry Keusch
Portland Middle School

John Manzini
Portland Middle School

Mary Parker
Portland Middle School

Scott Sandborn
Portland Middle School

Shepherd

Steve Brant
Shepherd Middle School

Marty Brock
Shepherd Middle School

Cathy Church
Shepherd Middle School

Ginny Crandall
Shepherd Middle School

Craig Ericksen
Shepherd Middle School

Natalie Hackney
Shepherd Middle School

Bill Hamilton
Shepherd Middle School

Julie Salisbury
Shepherd Middle School

Sturgis

Sandra Allen
Eastwood Elementary School

Margaret Baker
Eastwood Elementary School

Steven Baker
Eastwood Elementary School

Keith Barnes
Sturgis Middle School

Wilodean Beckwith
Eastwood Elementary School

Darcy Bird
Eastwood Elementary School

Bill Dickey
Sturgis Middle School

Ellen Eisele
Sturgis Middle School

James Hoelscher
Sturgis Middle School

Richard Nolan
Sturgis Middle School

J. Hunter Raiford
Sturgis Middle School

Cindy Sprowl
Eastwood Elementary School

Leslie Stewart
Eastwood Elementary School

Connie Sutton
Eastwood Elementary School

Traverse City

Maureen Bauer
Interlochen Elementary School

Ivanka Berskshire
East Junior High School

Sarah Boehm
Courtade Elementary School

Marilyn Conklin
Interlochen Elementary School

Nancy Crandall
Blair Elementary School

Fran Cullen
Courtade Elementary School

Eric Dreier
Old Mission Elementary School

Lisa Dzierwa
Cherry Knoll Elementary School

Ray Fouch
West Junior High School

Ed Hargis
Willow Hill Elementary School

Richard Henry
West Junior High School

Dessie Hughes
Cherry Knoll Elementary School

Ruthanne Kladder
Oak Park Elementary School

Bonnie Knapp
West Junior High School

Sue Laisure
Sabin Elementary School

Stan Malaski
Oak Park Elementary School

Jody Meyers
Sabin Elementary School

Marsha Myles
East Junior High School

Mary Beth O'Neil
Traverse Heights Elementary School

Jan Palkowski
East Junior High School

Karen Richardson
Old Mission Elementary School

Kristin Sak
Bertha Vos Elementary School

Mary Beth Schmitt
East Junior High School

Mike Schrotenboer
Norris Elementary School

Gail Smith
Willow Hill Elementary School

Karrie Tufts
Eastern Elementary School

Mike Wilson
East Junior High School

Tom Wilson
West Junior High School

Minnesota

Minneapolis

Betsy Ford
Northeast Middle School

New York

East Elmhurst

Allison Clark
Louis Armstrong Middle School

Dorothy Hershey
Louis Armstrong Middle School

J. Lewis McNeece
Louis Armstrong Middle School

Rossana Perez
Louis Armstrong Middle School

Merna Porter
Louis Armstrong Middle School

Marie Turini
Louis Armstrong Middle School

North Carolina

Durham

Everly Broadway
Durham Public Schools

Thomas Carson
Duke School for Children

Mary Hebrank
Duke School for Children

Bill O'Connor
Duke School for Children

Ruth Pershing
Duke School for Children

Peter Reichert
Duke School for Children

Elizabeth City

Rita Banks
Elizabeth City Middle School

Beth Chaundry
Elizabeth City Middle School

Amy Cuthbertson
Elizabeth City Middle School

Deni Dennison
Elizabeth City Middle School

Jean Gray
Elizabeth City Middle School

John McMenamin
Elizabeth City Middle School

Nicollette Nixon
Elizabeth City Middle School

Malinda Norfleet
Elizabeth City Middle School

Joyce O'Neal
Elizabeth City Middle School

Clevie Sawyer
Elizabeth City Middle School

Juanita Shannon
Elizabeth City Middle School

Terry Thorne
Elizabeth City Middle School

Rebecca Wardour
Elizabeth City Middle School

Leora Winslow
Elizabeth City Middle School

Franklinton

Susan Haywood
Franklinton Elementary School

Clyde Melton
Franklinton Elementary School

Louisburg

Lisa Anderson
Terrell Lane Middle School

Jackie Frazier
Terrell Lane Middle School

Pam Harris
Terrell Lane Middle School

Ohio

Toledo

Bonnie Bias
Hawkins Elementary School

Marsha Jackish
Hawkins Elementary School

Lee Jagodzinski
DeVeaux Junior High School

Norma J. King
Old Orchard Elementary School

Margaret McCready
Old Orchard Elementary School

Carmella Morton
DeVeaux Junior High School

Karen C. Rohrs
Hawkins Elementary School

Marie Sahloff
DeVeaux Junior High School

L. Michael Vince
McTigue Junior High School

Brenda D. Watkins
Old Orchard Elementary School

Oregon

Canby

Sandra Kralovec
Ackerman Middle School

Portland

Roberta Cohen
Catlin Gabel School

David Ellenberg
Catlin Gabel School

Sara Normington
Catlin Gabel School

Karen Scholte-Arce
Catlin Gabel School

West Linn

Marge Burack
Wood Middle School

Tracy Wygant
Athey Creek Middle School

Pennsylvania

Pittsburgh

Sheryl Adams
Reizenstein Middle School

Sue Barie
Frick International Studies Academy

Suzie Berry
Frick International Studies Academy

Richard Delgrosso
Frick International Studies Academy

Janet Falkowski
Frick International Studies Academy

Joanne George
Reizenstein Middle School

Harriet Hopper
Reizenstein Middle School

Chuck Jessen
Reizenstein Middle School

Ken Labuskes
Reizenstein Middle School

Barbara Lewis
Reizenstein Middle School

Sharon Mihalich
Reizenstein Middle School

Marianne O'Connor
Frick International Studies Academy

Mark Sammartino
Reizenstein Middle School

Washington

Seattle

Chris Johnson
University Preparatory Academy

Rick Purn
University Preparatory Academy

Contents

Mathematical questions often begin with the words *how many* or *how much*: How many different automobile license plates are possible in a state that prints license plates using the form ABC 123? How much time would it take to open a combination lock by trying all possible combinations?

To answer such questions, one must be able to count and to use the operations of addition, subtraction, multiplication, and division. Calculators have made performing arithmetic operations easy, but the user must know which operations to use and when to use them.

The primary goal of this unit is to help students learn some new and very useful strategies for reasoning in situations that involve counting possibilities. In the process, students are given many opportunities to review concepts from previous units, to develop mental-estimation skills, to practice important problem-solving strategies, and to talk and write about mathematical ideas and procedures.

The concepts, skills, and problem-solving goals of this unit are developed in a series of investigations fashioned around the story of a robbery. The investigating detective is faced with several mathematical puzzles as she considers the various pieces of evidence. The questions she asks fit two basic patterns:

How many ways could _____ happen?

How long would it take for _____ to happen?

Students develop and apply strategies for counting combinations of whole numbers, letters, and other denumerable items to answer these types of questions. Each problem presents either another experience within a new context or another variation of a previous counting problem, such as not permitting repeats or considering order variations as identical.

From this diverse set of experiences, students will develop a sense of the structure of problems involving counting. They will also learn to consider the special circumstances of various counting situations, such as whether or not order is important.

In assessing student learning in *Clever Counting,* it is critical to pose questions that require students to analyze patterns and to search for strategies for counting the number of possibilities. Students are expected to have ready access to calculators to perform arithmetic operations, so they can focus on the problem-analysis and pattern-search aspects of mathematics. They should be asked to demonstrate that they know how to model a problem successfully, using an organized list, a diagram, or some other representation that captures the essence of the number of choices.

The answers to most counting questions require multiplying and dividing whole numbers. However, it is not usually obvious *which* numbers should be multiplied or divided. In this unit, students will further develop their understanding of when multiplication and division can be used to solve problems. They will see how important problem-solving strategies, such as looking for patterns or making diagrams and organized lists of possibilities, can help in analyzing the structure of a problem situation.

Combinatorics

The study of counting methods is called *combinatorics*. The issue of whether order is important is the central difference between *permutations* and *combinations*. These concepts are used in the study of probability.

A *permutation* is an ordered arrangement of elements selected from a larger set of elements. If you select *r* elements from a set of *n* elements (with repeats not allowed), there are

$$n(n-1)(n-2) \cdots (n-r+1)$$

ways to make the selection if order matters.

A *combination* is a subset of a set of elements. The order in which the elements of the subset are listed does not matter. If you select a subset of *r* elements from a set of *n* elements (with repeats not allowed), there are

$$\frac{n(n-1)(n-2) \cdots (n-r+1)}{r(r-1)(r-2) \cdots (1)}$$

ways to choose an unordered set. The denominator of *r*! divides out the repetitions of arrangements of *r* elements.

Counting Possibilities

In Problem 2.2, students explore how many possible combinations exist for a standard combination lock. For the lock pictured here, there are 59,280 possible three-number combinations if a number may not be repeated in a combination.

This number can be determined by reasoning as follows:

■ There are 40 choices for the first number.

■ For each of those 40 choices, there are 39 choices for the second number, giving
  $40 \times 39 = 1560$ possibilities for the first two numbers.

■ For each of those 1560 possibilities, there are 38 choices for the third number, giving
  $1560 \times 38 = 59{,}280$ possible three-number combinations.

This type of reasoning will not be obvious to students initially. Simpler cases can be analyzed to generate data and patterns that will reveal shortcut counting strategies. Consider a lock with only three numbers on its dial, 0, 1, 2, and repeats in a combination not allowed. An organized list reveals that there are six possible three-number combinations:

0-1-2   0-2-1   1-0-2   1-2-0   2-0-1   2-1-0

A counting tree can be constructed for this situation as well.

First number	Second number	Third number	Combination
0	1	2	0-1-2
	2	1	0-2-1
1	0	2	1-0-2
	2	0	1-2-0
2	0	1	2-0-1
	1	0	2-1-0

start

If repeats *are* allowed, the number of possible combinations is much greater. An organized list might look like this:

0-0-0	0-1-0	0-2-0
0-0-1	0-1-1	0-2-1
0-0-2	0-1-2	0-2-2
1-0-0	1-1-0	1-2-0
1-0-1	1-1-1	1-2-1
1-0-2	1-1-2	1-2-2
2-0-0	2-1-0	2-2-0
2-0-1	2-1-1	2-2-1
2-0-2	2-1-2	2-2-2

A counting tree also reveals that there are 27 possible combinations:

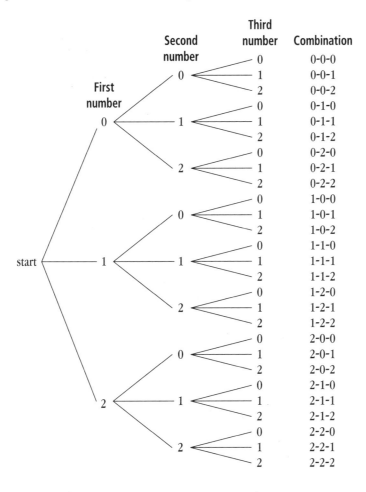

		Third	
	Second	number	Combination
First	number	0	0-0-0
number	0	1	0-0-1
		2	0-0-2

First number	Second number	Third number	Combination
0	0	0	0-0-0
		1	0-0-1
		2	0-0-2
	1	0	0-1-0
		1	0-1-1
		2	0-1-2
	2	0	0-2-0
		1	0-2-1
		2	0-2-2
1	0	0	1-0-0
		1	1-0-1
		2	1-0-2
	1	0	1-1-0
		1	1-1-1
		2	1-1-2
	2	0	1-2-0
		1	1-2-1
		2	1-2-2
2	0	0	2-0-0
		1	2-0-1
		2	2-0-2
	1	0	2-1-0
		1	2-1-1
		2	2-1-2
	2	0	2-2-0
		1	2-2-1
		2	2-2-2

Students are already familiar with these techniques; this is an opportunity for them to use organized lists and counting trees in a new context. The patterns in lists and counting trees offer clues that multiplication is the key to solving such counting problems.

The Fundamental Counting Principle

Consider the organized lists and counting trees for the combination lock with three marks. If repeats are not allowed, there are three choices for the first number in the combination, two choices for the second, and only one for the third. This implies that there are $3 \times 2 \times 1$ (or 3!) possible combinations. If repeats are allowed, there are three groups of three groups of three, as seen in the list or the tree. This leads to $3 \times 3 \times 3$ as the expression representing the number of possible combinations.

Students should be able to apply their knowledge of algebra to express these patterns generally and to explain why the number of combinations does not increase in a linear fashion as the number of choices increases. For a standard combination lock, there are $40 \times 39 \times 38$ possible combinations. The impact of the number of positions and the number of choices for each position can be analyzed. Such an analysis leads to the *fundamental counting principle:*

> If a sequence of actions, *a, b, c,* and so on, will produce an outcome and the outcome consists of one option from the available choices for each action, then the number of possible outcomes can be computed by multiplying the number of choices for each action. For example, if action *a* can be accomplished in 4 ways, action *b* in 10 ways, and action *c* in 3 ways, there are $4 \times 10 \times 3$ possible outcomes consisting of one of the choices for each of *a, b,* and *c.*

Networks

Investigation 3 introduces some ideas from graph theory. In this new context, students make connections between the strategies they have developed to count lock combinations and counting the number of different paths through a network.

The simple network below has three nodes, A, B, and C, which might represent towns or intersections. There are two edges from node A to node B and five edges from node B to node C. To answer the question of how many different paths there are from node A to node C through node B, we could label the edges from node A to node B and from node B to node C and make an organized list. We could make a counting tree to show all the possibilities. Or we could use the fundamental counting principle: the total number of paths from node A to node C through node B is $2 \times 5 = 10$.

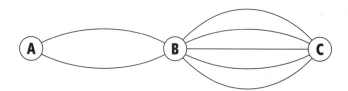

The Consideration of Order

When students have become comfortable looking for the facts that determine how many positions there are, how many choices exist for each position, and whether or not repeats are allowed, the problems change subtly, introducing the idea of order. Now, for example, 0-1 and 1-0 are considered to be the same sequence. Students must modify their counting strategies to account for the repetitions.

For example, when counting all the different dominoes in a set, students must adjust for the fact that their usual strategy—seven possible choices in each of two positions—will not work; a 2-6 domino is the same as a 6-2 domino. Or, when two objects are chosen from a set of six, whether a particular object is chosen first or second does not matter: choosing a blue, a green, and a red marble is equivalent to choosing a red, a blue, and a green marble. This kind of problem is not generalized algebraically in this unit, but stays at the list-and-count level.

Connected Mathematics™ was developed with the belief that calculators should always be available and that students should decide when to use them. Most of the calculations in *Clever Counting* can be done on a simple four-function calculator. However, students are occasionally asked to relate the patterns they discover to algebraic relationships they have seen, and a graphing calculator can assist in this exploration.

Calculating Factorials

Several problems in this unit eventually lead to the calculation of a factorial, $n!$, the multiplication of all positive integers up to and including n. The term is introduced in the student edition in the ACE section of Investigation 2.

To use the factorial function on the TI-80 graphing calculator, first enter the value. Then display the MATH PRB menu, which looks like the screen shown below left, by pressing MATH. Select PRB (probability) and choice 4 to select !, factorial. For example, the number of four-number combinations with no repeats that can be made from four numbers is $4 \times 3 \times 2 \times 1$. To evaluate this, enter 4 and choose the factorial function.

```
MATH  NUM  PRB
1:RAND
2:nPr
3:nCr
4:!
5:RANDINT(
```

```
4!
              24
```

Mathematical and Problem-Solving Goals

C*lever Counting* **was created to help students**

- Recognize situations in which counting techniques apply

- Construct organized lists of outcomes for complex processes and uncover patterns that help in counting the outcomes of those processes

- Use diagrams, tables, and symbolic expressions to organize examples in listing and counting tasks

- Analyze the usefulness of counting trees and use counting trees

- Use mental arithmetic to make estimates in multiplication and division calculations

- Invent strategies for solving problems that involve counting

- Analyze counting problems involving choices in various contexts

- Differentiate among situations in which order does and does not matter and in which repeats are and are not allowed

- Analyze the number of paths through a network

- Compare the structures of networks with problems involving combinations

- Create networks that satisfy given constraints

- Apply thinking and reasoning skills to an open-ended situation in which assumptions must be made and create a persuasive argument to support a conjecture

The overall goal of the Connected Mathematics curriculum is to help students develop sound mathematical habits. Through their work in this and other units, students learn important questions to ask themselves about any situation that can be represented and modeled mathematically, such as: *What are the variables? How are they changing in relation to each other? How is an increase in the independent variable related to a change in the dependent variable? How can this change be seen in a table? Detected in a story? Observed in a graph? Read from symbolic representation?*

Clever Counting poses additional questions that students learn to ask themselves, such as: *Is this a situation in which a sequence of actions must take place to produce an outcome? What are the constraints on the situation? Can an option be used repeatedly, or are repeats not allowed? Does order matter? Is multiplication an appropriate solution method? If so, what do I multiply to model the number of possibilities in the situation? How do I know that my model is reasonable? Would a counting tree help me to organize my thinking? Would starting an organized list of possibilities help me?*

Investigation 1: Counting Possibilities

The main theme of the unit, counting by using multiplication, is introduced. The basic problem form—whether it is combinations of facial features or numbers on license plates, telephone numbers, or zip codes—is a sequence constructed by making a choice for each element in the sequence. If there are a ways to fill the first position, b ways to fill the second, c ways to fill the third, and so on, there will be $a \times b \times c \times \cdots$ possible sequences. Students first consider a problem that has only a few outcomes and that can be easily modeled with an organized list or a counting tree. The second problem involves many more possibilities, encouraging students to search for patterns that will help them solve the problem by reasoning rather than by listing all the possibilities.

Investigation 2: Opening Locks

By investigating the number of possible combinations for two kinds of locks—push-button locks and standard combination locks—students become aware of some fundamental properties of counting that can be found in situations that, on the surface, seem unrelated. The mathematical analyses of the two situations are similar: characters cannot be repeated in a combination, and the counting of possible combinations can be expedited by multiplication.

Investigation 3: Networks

Students explore a common counting application: finding the number of paths through a network. Networks offer visual representations of the multiplication technique, which can be applied to many other multistep processes. The basic idea of counting paths is that the number of ways to get from point A to point C via point B is the product of the number of paths from A to B and the number of paths from B to C. The words *network, node,* and *edge* are introduced to make it easier for students to communicate about such diagrams. Students are also asked to create networks that satisfy given constraints.

Investigation 4: Deciding Whether Order Is Important

Students discover that, in each counting situation they encounter, they must consider whether order is important. The context of a problem is crucial, as it determines whether possibilities such as 1-2 and 2-1 are to be counted as the same outcome or different outcomes. Students consider two situations in which order does not matter. First they analyze how many different double-six dominoes there are. Students often initially approach this problem using familiar, but erroneous, reasoning: there are seven possible dot, or pip, arrangements on each half of a domino, so there ought to be $7 \times 7 = 49$ different dominoes. This reasoning overlooks the fact that domino halves are not ordered as first and second, and students must think about the situation more carefully. They then analyze a second situation in which order is not important: selecting a set of objects from a larger collection.

Investigation 5: Wrapping Things Up

This open-ended investigation offers a review and a summary of the ideas students have encountered in *Clever Counting*. Drawing on what they have learned about counting in the previous investigations, students are encouraged to ask and answer more sophisticated questions and to have fun speculating about the many ways they can apply their newfound reasoning.

The ideas in *Clever Counting* build on and connect to several big ideas in other Connected Mathematics units.

Big Idea	Prior Work	Future Work
understanding and comparing large numbers	scaling quantities and objects up and down; comparing quantities expressed as decimals, percents, and fractions; and comparing categorical and numerical data *(Data About Us; Bits and Pieces II; Comparing and Scaling; Filling and Wrapping; Data Around Us)*	continuing the study of counting, graph theory, and probability *(high school)*
constructing organized lists and counting trees to enumerate possibilities	listing all possible outcomes *(How Likely Is It?; What Do You Expect?)* finding all the rectangles and prisms that fit given constraints *(Covering and Surrounding; Filling and Wrapping)* making factor trees to find prime factorizations *(Prime Time)*	continuing the study of counting, graph theory, and probability *(high school)* continuing the study of number theory *(high school)*
recognizing patterns, generalizing patterns, and using patterns to make predictions	looking for regularity and making predictions (virtually every unit provides these opportunities; the algebra units are especially rich: *Variables and Patterns; Moving Straight Ahead; Thinking with Mathematical Models; Looking for Pythagoras; Growing, Growing, Growing; Frogs, Fleas, and Painted Cubes; Say It with Symbols)*	making inferences and predictions based on observing patterns and proving the existence of patterns *(high school and beyond)*

Big Idea	Prior Work	Future Work
recognizing situations that call for multiplication or division	developing algorithms for performing calculations with fractions, decimals, and percents *(Bits and Pieces I; Bits and Pieces II)* applying knowledge of ratio, proportion, and percent *(Comparing and Scaling)* understanding the multiplicative structure of numbers *(Prime Time; Covering and Surrounding; Filling and Wrapping; Data Around Us)*	continuing the study of counting, graph theory, and probability *(high school)* continuing the study of number theory *(high school)*
inventing and using the fundamental counting principle	understanding the multiplicative structure of numbers *(Prime Time; Covering and Surrounding; Filling and Wrapping; Data Around Us)*	continuing the study of counting, graph theory, and probability *(high school)* continuing the study of number theory *(high school)*

Materials

For students

- Labsheet UP (optional; 1 per student)
- Graphing calculators (preferably with the capacity to display a function as a table)
- Large sheets of paper (optional)
- Cuisenaire® rods (optional, for the Unit Project; as many as are available)

For the teacher

- Transparencies and transparency markers (optional)
- Overhead display model of students' graphing calculators (optional)
- Combination lock (optional)
- License plate (optional)
- Set of dominoes or set of overhead dominoes (provided as a blackline master)

Resources

Corbet, James J., and J. Susan Milton. "Who Killed the Cook?" *Mathematics Teacher* (April 1978): 263–66.

Cozzens, Margaret B., and Richard D. Porter. *Problem Solving Using Graphs*. Arlington, Mass.: COMAP, 1987.

Kappraff, Jay. *Connections: The Geometric Bridge Between Art and Science*. New York: McGraw-Hill, 1991.

Kenney, Margaret, and Christian Hirsch, eds. *Discrete Mathematics Across the Curriculum K–12*. Reston, Va.: NCTM, 1991.

Landauer, Edwin. "Counting Using License Plates and Phone Numbers." *Mathematics Teacher* (March 1984): 183–87.

Messer, Robert. "Factorial!" *Mathematics Teacher* (January 1984): 50–51.

Perham, Bernadette, and Arnold Perham. *Graph Theory*. Menlo Park, Calif.: Addison-Wesley, 1993.

Succo, William; Wayne Copes; Clifford Sloyer; and Robert Stark. *Graph Theory: Euler's Rich Legacy*. Providence, R.I.: Janson Publications, 1987.

Pacing Chart

This pacing chart gives estimates of the class time required for each investigation and assessment piece. Shaded rows indicate opportunities for assessment.

Investigations and Assessments	Class Time
1 Counting Possibilities	3 days
2 Opening Locks	4 days
Check-Up	$\frac{1}{2}$ day
3 Networks	3 days
4 Deciding Whether Order Is Important	3 days
Quiz	1 day
5 Wrapping Things Up	2 days
Self-Assessment	Take home
Unit Test	1 day
Optional Unit Project	1 day

Clever Counting Vocabulary

The following words and concepts are used in *Clever Counting*. Concepts in the left column are those essential for student understanding of this unit. The Descriptive Glossary gives descriptions of some of these terms.

Essential terms developed in this unit
counting tree
edge
network
node

Terms developed in previous units
organized list
probability

Embedded Assessment

Opportunities for informal assessment of student progress are embedded throughout *Clever Counting* in the problems, the ACE questions, and the Mathematical Reflections. Suggestions for observing as students explore and discover mathematical ideas, for probing to guide their progress in developing concepts and skills, and for questioning to determine their level of understanding can be found in the Launch, Explore, and Summarize sections of all investigation problems. Some examples:

- Investigation 1, Problem 1.2 *Launch* (page 14c) suggests a way to introduce students to the idea of determining how many possible combinations exist in a counting situation.
- Investigation 2, Problem 2.2 *Explore* (page 26c) suggests ideas for helping to guide students in reasoning about how many possible combinations there are for a combination lock.
- Investigation 4, Problem 4.2 *Summarize* (page 46d) suggests questions you can ask to assess and extend students' understanding of the patterns underlying counting situations in which order is not important and repeats are not allowed.

ACE Assignments

An ACE (Applications—Connections—Extensions) section appears at the end of each investigation. To help you assign ACE questions, a list of assignment choices is given in the margin next to the reduced student page for each problem. Each list indicates the ACE questions that students should be able to answer after they complete the problem.

Check-Up

One check-up, which may be given after Investigation 2, is provided for use as a quick quiz or warm-up activity. The check-up is designed for students to complete individually. You will find the check-up and its answer key in the Assessment Resources section.

Partner Quiz

One quiz, which may be given after Investigation 4, is provided with this unit. The quiz is designed to be completed by pairs of students with the opportunity for revision based on teacher feedback. You will find the quiz and its answer key in the Assessment Resources section. As an alternative to the quiz provided, you can construct your own quiz by combining questions from the Question Bank, this quiz, and unassigned ACE questions.

Question Bank

A Question Bank provides questions you can use for homework, reviews, or quizzes. You will find the Question Bank and its answer key in the Assessment Resources section.

Notebook/Journal

Students should have notebooks to record and organize their work. Notebooks should include student journals and sections for vocabulary, homework, quizzes, and check-ups. In their journals, students can take notes, solve investigation problems, and record their ideas about Mathematical Reflections questions. Journals should be assessed for completeness rather than correctness; they should be seen as "safe" places where students can try out their thinking. A Notebook Checklist and a Self-Assessment are provided in the Assessment Resources section. The Notebook Checklist helps students organize their notebooks. The Self-Assessment guides students as they review their notebooks to determine which ideas they have mastered and which they still need to work on.

The Unit Test

The final assessment in *Clever Counting* is a unit test that focuses on examining a range of counting situations, including situations in which order is important, in which order is not important, in which the multiplication technique is useful, and in which the multiplication technique is not useful. Alternatively, the first unit project—Project 1, Writing a Detective Story—can be used as the final assessment, as students will need to review all they have learned about counting to create the situations in their detective stories.

The Optional Unit Project

Clever Counting includes two optional unit projects. Project 1, Writing a Detective Story, gives students an opportunity to apply what they have learned about counting in a creative way and is comprehensive enough to be used as the final assessment of the unit. Project 2, Making Chains, combines students' prior knowledge of patterns and equations with what they have learned in this unit about counting. Though not a comprehensive assessment of all students have learned, the project does offer students a complex problem to which they can apply their new counting tools. Descriptions and guides for assessment are given in the Assessment Resources section.

Introducing Your Students to *Clever Counting*

To introduce your students to *Clever Counting*, read the story of the locker robbery and have students consider these questions: *Whom do you suspect? What questions would you like to ask Rodney? What questions would you like to ask the manager, the night guard, the guard's friend, or the detective?*

One of the most intriguing questions in this case is whether the guard could have opened the locker without knowing the combination of its lock. Some students will focus on this issue quickly and attempt to analyze the possibilities. Some may not identify this question as critical, and others will not be able to arrive at answers that they can convincingly justify. All of these reactions are fine; the goal here is to hook the students into the story and to help them articulate their beginning suspicions and questions.

Clever Counting

A locker at a storage warehouse was robbed. The police suspect that the thief tried possible lock combinations until the lock opened. A lock combination consists of three numbers from 0 to 39, with no repeated numbers. How many combinations are possible?

A witness saw a white van speed away from the scene of a crime. He said the van had in-state license plates starting with the letters MTU. License plates in the state where the robbery took place contain three letters followed by three numbers. How many possible plates start with MTU?

A domino is a rectangular tile divided into halves. On a standard double-six domino, each half contains from 0 to 6 dots, called pips. A complete set of dominoes contains one domino for each possible combination of halves. How many dominoes are in a complete set?

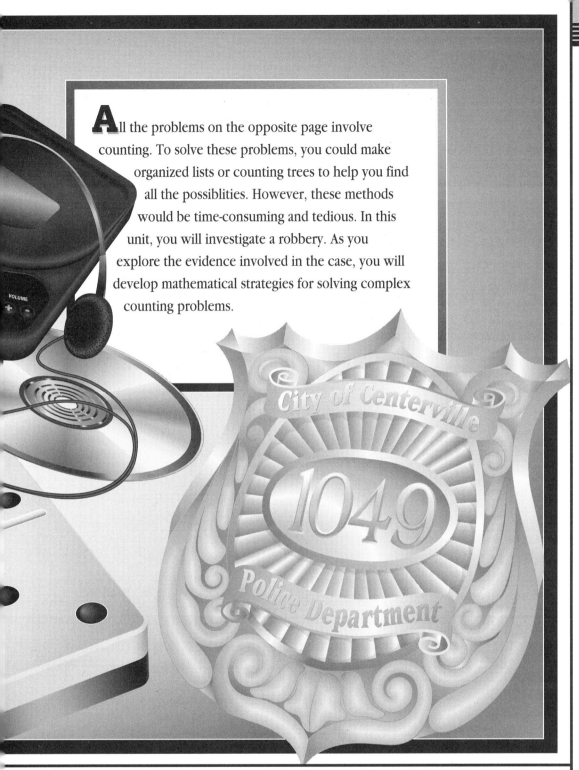

All the problems on the opposite page involve counting. To solve these problems, you could make organized lists or counting trees to help you find all the possiblities. However, these methods would be time-consuming and tedious. In this unit, you will investigate a robbery. As you explore the evidence involved in the case, you will develop mathematical strategies for solving complex counting problems.

City of Centerville

1049

Police Department

Other clues that the detective has gathered indicate additional complications, such as the patrol of the warehouse and the suspicious van that raced from the parking lot. Real life does not supply neatly packaged questions, and students may experience some frustration because they do not know what is significant and they do not have all the details. Making a list of "need to know" questions from this introductory discussion will set the tone for the rest of the unit. Each investigation will add more clarification and more detail.

Mathematical Highlights

The Mathematical Highlights page provides information to students and to parents and other family members. It gives students a preview of the activities and problems in *Clever Counting*. As they work through the unit, students can refer back to the Mathematical Highlights page to review what they have learned and to preview what is still to come. This page also tells students' families what mathematical ideas and activities will be covered as the class works through *Clever Counting*.

Mathematical Highlights

In *Clever Counting*, you will investigate a robbery. As you work through the unit, you will learn techniques for solving problems that involve counting.

- As you explore the possible faces a police artist can draw and the possible license plates with a given sequence of characters, you begin to develop counting strategies.

- Finding the number of possible combinations for push-button locks and combination locks helps you discover an important counting principle.

- As you explore the possible paths a security guard might follow on her rounds, you are introduced to networks.

- Designing networks meeting given constraints leads you to discover the relationship between the number of edges connecting each pair of nodes in a network and the total number of paths through the network.

- Finding the number of dominoes in a set helps you see that in some counting situations, order is not important.

Using a Calculator

In this unit, you might use the factorial function on your calculator to help you solve counting problems. As you work on the Connected Mathematics™ units, you will decide whether to use a calculator to help you solve a problem.

The Investigations

The teaching materials for each investigation consist of three parts: an overview, student pages with teaching outlines, and detailed notes for teaching the investigation.

The overview of each investigation includes brief descriptions of the problems, the mathematical and problem-solving goals of the investigation, and a list of necessary materials.

Essential information for teaching the investigation is provided in the margins around the student pages. The "At a Glance" overviews are brief outlines of the Launch, Explore, and Summarize phases of each problem for reference as you work with the class. To help you assign homework, a list of "Assignment Choices" is provided next to each problem. Where space permits, answers to problems, follow-ups, ACE questions, and Mathematical Reflections appear next to the appropriate student pages.

The Teaching the Investigation section follows the student pages and is the heart of the Connected Mathematics curriculum. This section describes in detail the Launch, Explore, and Summarize phases for each problem. It includes all the information needed for teaching, along with suggestions for what you might say at key points in the teaching. Use this section to prepare lessons and as a guide for teaching the investigations.

Assessment Resources

The Assessment Resources section contains blackline masters and answer keys for the check-up, the quiz, the Question Bank, and the Unit Test. It also provides guidelines for assessing the optional unit project. Blackline masters for the Notebook Checklist and the Self-Assessment are given. These instruments support student self-evaluation, an important aspect of assessment in the Connected Mathematics curriculum. Guides for assessing students' work on the check-up and the quiz are also included.

Blackline Masters

The Blackline Masters section includes masters for all labsheets and transparencies.

Additional Practice

Practice pages for each investigation offer additional problems for students who need more practice with the basic concepts developed in the investigations as well as some continual review of earlier concepts.

Descriptive Glossary

The glossary provides descriptions and examples of the key concepts in *Clever Counting*. These descriptions are not intended to be formal definitions but are meant to give you an idea of how students might make sense of these important concepts.

Counting Possibilities

The two problems in this investigation introduce the main theme of the unit: counting by using multiplication. The basic counting problem—whether it involves combinations of facial features or numbers on license plates, telephone numbers, or postal zip codes—consists of a sequence constructed by making a choice for each element of the sequence. If there are a ways to fill the first position, b ways to fill the second position, c ways to fill the third position, and so on, there will be $a \times b \times c \times \cdots$ different possible sequences.

The unit has several cognitive objectives. Students will begin developing the habit of constructing examples to fit a set of conditions and then looking for patterns in those examples. They will compare the structures of different problems, looking for similarities and differences. And they will reflect on the strategies and representations they used and evaluate their usefulness.

Rather than suggesting a particular solution strategy, Problem 1.1, Making Faces, offers students an opportunity to invent ways to understand and model the possible choices. In Problem 1.2, Checking Plate Numbers, students consider how many license plates are possible, given certain combinations of letters and digits. Using multiplication is one appropriate solution strategy.

Mathematical and Problem-Solving Goals

- *To analyze counting problems involving choices in different contexts*

- *To analyze the usefulness of counting trees*

- *To use counting trees*

- *To begin to see a connection between some counting situations and the operation of multiplication*

Materials		
Problem	**For students**	**For the teacher**
All	Graphing calculators	Transparencies: 1.1 and 1.2 (optional)
1.1	Large sheets of paper (optional)	
1.2		License plate (optional)

Counting Possibilities

Rodney's Radical Sounds sells radios, tape decks, and compact disc players at discount prices. There is very little room in the store to keep merchandise that is not on display, so Rodney rents a storage locker at the nearby Fail-Safe storage warehouse.

One afternoon, Rodney went to his locker and discovered that a box of expensive compact disc players was missing. He called the police, and Detective Ima Curious came to investigate.

During her initial investigation, Detective Curious gathered the following information:

*   There were no signs of forced entry, and the only fingerprints on the locker were Rodney's.
*   Rodney had visited his locker at noon the day before, and nothing was missing.
*   The warehouse manager is on duty from 9 A.M. to 6 P.M. every day.

Investigation 1: Counting Possibilities **5**

Tips for the Linguistically Diverse Classroom

Enactment The Enactment technique is described in detail in *Getting to Know Connected Mathematics*. Students act out mini-scenes using props to make information comprehensible. Example: For the information presented on this page, students can assume the roles of Rodney and the warehouse manager, using a shoe box to represent the box of compact disc players. The enactment can begin with Rodney pantomiming opening his locker and pulling out the box of disk players as the teacher writes yesterday's date and *12:00 noon* on the board. Another student could pantomime the manager strolling by, checking all around, as the teacher records his hours on duty on the board and writes the current date next to yesterday's date to show that time has passed. Rodney can then again visit the locker, this time showing surprise upon discovering the empty box, and role-play calling the police.

Making Faces

Grouping:
individuals or pairs

Launch

- Introduce the story of the robbery.

- Talk about the police artist's list of features.

- Have students work individually or in pairs on the problem and follow-up.

Explore

- If students are struggling, ask whether making an organized list or a counting tree would be helpful.

- Distribute large sheets of paper for some students to record answers. *(optional)*

Summarize

- Ask students to share their solution strategies.

- Discuss the follow-up.

Assignment Choices

ACE questions 1, 2, 4, 5, 13, and 14

- Some of the lockers at Fail-Safe have push-button locks; others have combination locks. The manager keeps a list of all the combinations hidden in his office.

- The night security guard was on duty from 9 P.M. to 6 A.M. The manager suspects that the guard committed the robbery. He thinks the guard tried various combinations until the lock opened.

- The security guard said that, although she makes frequent rounds of the warehouse to inspect the locks and doors, she does not pass every locker on every trip through the warehouse.

- The security guard admitted that she was visited by a friend from 9:30 P.M. until about 11:30 P.M. She and her friend played dominoes for about an hour. After the friend left, the guard conducted a half-hour check of the warehouse.

- The guard's friend said that as he was leaving the warehouse, a van raced out of the parking lot with its lights off. He thought this was odd, so he tried to read the license plate. He could see that it was an in-state plate and contained the letters MTU, in that order. As the van passed under a street light, the friend caught a glimpse of the driver. He is certain the driver was a man.

Think about this!

Based on this information, whom, if anyone, do you suspect of committing the robbery? What questions would you like to ask Rodney, the manager, the night guard, the guard's friend, or the detective?

1.1 Making Faces

Detective Curious asked the guard's friend to work with a police artist to create a sketch of the man driving the van. To make an accurate sketch, the artist gave the witness choices for several facial features. For example, she asked, "What did his nose look like? Was it hooked? Long and straight? Turned up? Broken?"

Problem 1.1

Here are the choices the artist gave the witness:

Hair	Eyes	Nose
bushy	staring	hooked
bald	beady	long and straight
	droopy	turned up
	wide open	broken

A. How many facial descriptions can you make by choosing one attribute for each feature?

B. The witness said he remembered something distinctive about the driver's mouth. The artist suggested these possibilities:

Mouth
thin and mean
toothless
sinister grin

If you consider the hair, eyes, nose, and mouth, how many facial descriptions can you make by choosing one attribute for each feature?

Problem 1.1 Follow-Up

1. Of all the facial descriptions you found in part B, how many include droopy eyes?

2. Of all the facial descriptions you found in part B, how many include a bald head and a thin, mean mouth?

Answers to Problem 1.1

A. There are $2 \times 4 \times 4 = 32$ possible facial descriptions. See the "Explore" section for ways students might approach this problem.

B. There are $2 \times 4 \times 4 \times 3 = 96$ possible facial descriptions.

Answers to Problem 1.1 Follow-Up

1. With the choice for eyes set, only choices for hair, nose, and mouth matter, giving $2 \times 4 \times 3 = 24$ facial descriptions that include droopy eyes. (Students may count to find the possibilities rather than multiply.)

2. With the choices for hair and mouth set, only choices for eyes and nose matter, giving $4 \times 4 = 16$ facial descriptions that include bald heads and thin, mean mouths.

[Handwritten margin notes:] Does order matter when artist draws? no

FU 1.1.1 Suppose we knew eyes are droopy, how many possibilities? 1.1.2 What if you know 2 chars for sure? Suppose artist were to add 1 more chair to one list. Then eyes, nose, mouth) in which case is # possibilities largest? why.

Checking Plate Numbers

Grouping:
pairs

Launch

- Show or draw a license plate, and ask the class how many possibilities there are for each character on the plate.

- Have pairs work on the problem and follow-up.

Explore

- If students have trouble, suggest that they start a counting tree or an organized list and look for patterns.

Summarize

- Have students share how they reasoned about the problem.

- Help the class see that multiplication is an appropriate solution strategy.

1.2 Checking Plate Numbers

The witness claimed that he saw the license plate of the van. He said that it was an in-state plate containing the letter sequence MTU. In the state in which the robbery took place, license plates contain three letters followed by three numbers. How might this information help the detective solve her case?

Problem 1.2

Detective Curious wants to run each possible plate number through the computer to find out whether the registered owner has a criminal record. It takes about 20 seconds to check each plate number. How many possible plates start with MTU? Do you think this is a reasonable number of plates for the detective to check?

■ Problem 1.2 Follow-Up

1. When the detective questioned him a second time, the witness said he was really only sure that the first two letters of the plate were MT. How many possible license plates start with MT? How does this compare to the number of possible plates that start with MTU?

2. In a neighboring state, license plates have four letters followed by two numbers. Is the number of possible plates for this state greater than, less than, or equal to the number of possible plates for the state in which the crime took place? Explain your answer.

[handwritten notes: Does order matter? yes. 010 ≠ 100 Can you repeat digits? yes. How many #'s? 2 ways — 10·10·10 or #'s from 000 to 999. Suppose 4 digits. Suppose 3 letters. Use --- - slots. Compare facial chars prob vs. license plate prob.]

Assignment Choices

ACE questions 3, 6–12, 15–19, and unassigned choices from earlier problems

Answer to Problem 1.2

There are $10 \times 10 \times 10 = 1000$ possible license plates that start with MTU. Checking all of these plates would require $1000 \times 20 = 20,000$ seconds, or about 5.6 hours. Students may or may not think this amount of time is reasonable.

[handwritten: $20\,000 \cdot \frac{1}{60} \cdot \frac{1}{60} = \frac{20\,000}{3600} =$ secs min/sec, hr/min]

Answers to Problem 1.2 Follow-Up

1. With only two letters set, there are $26 \times 10 \times 10 \times 10 = 26,000$ possible license plates. This means there are $26,000 \div 1000 = 26$ times as many possibilities.

2. The number of possible plates for this state is greater; explanations will vary. There are $26^4 \times 10^2 = 45,697,600$ possible plates for that state; in the state in which the crime took place, there are $26^3 \times 10^3 = 17,576,000$ possible plates. Some students may reason that since there are 26 letters and only 10 digits, replacing the digit in the fourth position with a letter creates more possibilities.

Applications • Connections • Extensions

As you work on these ACE questions, use your calculator whenever you need it.

Applications

1. Makoto is getting dressed for school. The counting tree below shows his choices for shoes, pants, and shirts.

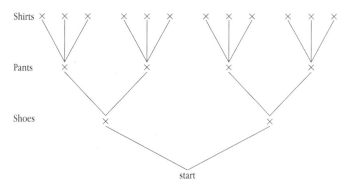

a. How many pairs of shoes does Makoto have to choose from?

b. How many pairs of pants does he have to choose from?

c. How many shirts does he have to choose from?

d. How many different combinations of shoes, pants, and a shirt can Makoto put together from these choices?

e. How can you find the answer to part d without counting each path in the diagram?

Answers

Applications

1a. 2

1b. 2 (For each choice of shoes, he can choose from 2 pairs of pants.)

1c. 3 (For each choice of pants, he can choose from 3 shirts.)

1d. There are 12 combinations.

1e. Count the number of entries in the top row, or compute $2 \times 2 \times 3$.

2. See page 14f.

3. There were 2 × 5 × 3 = 30 combinations. Students might show this with a counting tree. See below right.

4. This leaves 1 choice for hair, 3 choices for eyes, 3 choices for nose, and 2 choices for mouth, for 1 × 3 × 3 × 2 = 18 possible descriptions.

2. Ms. Suárez is choosy about what she eats. When she buys lunch in the company cafeteria, she considers only these options:

Main course	Drink	Dessert
salad	milk	fruit
pizza	orange juice	frozen yogurt
turkey sandwich		pie
		pudding

a. List four lunches Ms. Suárez might purchase. Each lunch should consist of one main course, one drink, and one dessert.

b. Copy and complete this tree diagram to show all the lunches Ms. Suárez might purchase.

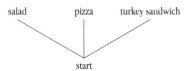

c. How many days can Ms. Suárez buy lunch in the cafeteria without having the same lunch twice?

3. At the meeting of the Future Teachers of America, ice cream cones were served. There were two kinds of cones, five flavors of ice cream, and three types of sprinkles. Each member chose one cone, one ice cream flavor, and one type of sprinkles. How many combinations were possible? Show your work.

4. Look back at the lists of hair, eyes, nose, and mouth attributes in Problem 1.1. The witness told the artist that he was sure the driver of the van was not bald. He was also certain that the driver did not have droopy eyes, a broken nose, or a sinister grin. If you eliminate these choices from the lists of attributes, how many descriptions can you make from the choices that remain?

10 **Clever Counting**

3. Sprinkles

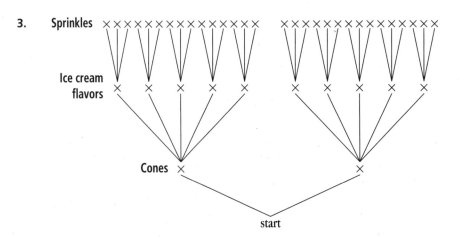

5. In a particular counting tree, four branches extend from the starting point. At the second level, five branches extend from each branch from the previous level. At the third level, three branches extend from each branch from the previous level. How many paths through the branches of the tree are possible?

6. License plates in the state where the locker robbery took place contain three letters followed by three numbers. In Problem 1.2, you found that this scheme provides enough plates for over 17 million cars. In states with small populations, such as Alaska, North Dakota, Wyoming, and Vermont, fewer than 1 million cars are registered.

    a. Suppose you are in charge of developing a license-plate scheme for a state with a million registered cars. Describe a scheme that would provide enough plates for all the cars and require the fewest characters.

    b. Can you think of another acceptable scheme that would use the same number of characters as the scheme you described in part a? Explain.

7. If a state's motorcycle plates contain four letters, such as ABCD or MIKE, how many plates are possible?

8. If a state's license plates contain three numbers followed by four letters, such as 543 JOHE or 112 BETY, how many plates are possible?

Connections

9. Suppose the witness remembers the three letters and the first two numbers of the van's license plate and guesses the last number. What is the probability that his guess will be correct? Explain your answer.

10. Suppose the witness recalls that the driver had bushy hair and beady eyes and guesses what his nose looked like. Can you determine the probability that his guess will be correct? Explain your answer.

5. Multiplying the branches at each level, there are $4 \times 5 \times 3 = 60$ paths.

6a. Possible schemes: Five letters would give $26^5 = 11,881,376$ license plates. Four letters followed by one number would give $26^4 \times 10 = 4,569,760$ license plates. Three letters followed by two numbers would give $26^3 \times 10^2 = 1,757,600$ license plates. Each scheme uses five characters.

6b. See answers to part a. In addition, the number-letter combinations could appear in any order, such as two letters followed by two numbers followed by a letter or two numbers followed by three letters.

7. $26^4 = 456,976$ possible plates

8. $10^3 \times 26^4 = 456,976,000$ possible plates

Connections

9. Since there are 10 possible digits for the last number and each is equally likely to be correct, the witness has a 1 in 10 chance, or a 10% probability, of guessing correctly.

10. It is not possible to determine the probability that his guess will be correct because the artist's four nose descriptions are probably not equally likely; we can't even assume that the driver's nose fits any of these descriptions.

11a. Answers will vary.

11b. 10^5 = 100,000 possible zip codes

11c. 10^9 = 1,000,000,000 possible zip+4 zip codes

11d. There are many more zip+4 zip codes than people (about 740 million more, or 1000 ÷ 260 ≈ 3.8 times as many).

12a. There are $26^3 \times 10^3$ = 17,576,000 possible plates.

i. 17,576,000 × 3 = 52,728,000 seconds

ii. 52,728,000 ÷ 60 = 878,800 minutes

iii. 878,800 ÷ 60 ≈ 14,647 hours

iv. 14,647 ÷ 24 ≈ 610 days

v. 610 ÷ 7 ≈ 87 weeks

vi. 610 ÷ 365 ≈ 1.7 years

12b. See below right.

12c. $p = 1200t$ or $t = \frac{p}{1200}$, where p is the number of plates produced in t hours (Note: The equation students write depends on whether they think in terms of how many plates are produced per hour or how much time it will take to produce a given number of plates.)

13a. A, H, I, M, O, T, U, V, W, X, and Y (Note: This property is called *reflection symmetry*.)

13b. There are 11 choices for each letter, for a total of 11^3 = 1331 combinations.

11. U.S. postal zip codes have two forms. The short form is a five-digit number, such as 54494. The longer form, called zip+4, has 9 digits, such as 48824-1027.

a. What is the short form for your zip code?

b. How many short-form zip codes are possible?

c. How many zip+4 zip codes are possible?

d. The U.S. population is about 260 million people. How does the number of possible zip+4 codes compare with the number of people in the United States?

12. a. Suppose it takes 3 seconds to manufacture a license plate. How much time would it take to manufacture every possible plate with three letters followed by three numbers? Assume the plates are made one at a time on a continuous production line. Express your answer in each of these units:

i. seconds   **ii.** minutes   **iii.** hours

iv. days   **v.** weeks   **vi.** years

b. Make a table and a graph to show how the manufacturing time in hours varies with the number of license plates produced.

c. Write an equation that shows how the manufacturing time relates to the number of license plates produced. Explain what each part of your equation means in terms of the situation.

13. If you held the letter U up to a mirror, its reflection would also be a U.

a. List all the capital letters with this reflection property.

b. The reflection of UTM in a mirror would be MTU. How many three-letter combinations have reflections that are also three-letter combinations?

12 **Clever Counting**

12b. The rate of production is 1 plate every 3 seconds, or 20 plates per minute, or 1200 plates per hour.

Time (hours)	Plates produced
0	0
1	1200
2	2400
3	3600
4	4800
5	6000
6	7200

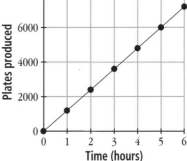

License-Plate Production

Extensions

14. In the Clue® board game, players try to solve a murder mystery. To win, a player must identify the murderer, the murder weapon, and the room in which the murder was committed. Amadi claims that there are 118 possible solutions to the game. His sister Ayana, who has never played the game, says she can't believe this is true. Why does she say this?

In 15–18, use a current almanac to help you answer the question.

15. In Texas, license plates have four letters followed by three numbers. What is the ratio of the number of possible plates to the state's population?

16. In Michigan, license plates have three letters followed by three numbers or three numbers followed by three letters. What is the ratio of the number of possible plates to the state's population?

17. In Alaska, license plates have three letters followed by three numbers. What is the ratio of the number of possible plates to the state's population?

18. In Utah, license plates have three letters followed by three numbers. What is the ratio of the number of possible plates to the state's population?

19. a. Suppose a country's postal codes consist of two characters. A code may have two letters, two numbers, or a letter and a number. How many two-character codes are possible? Consider A3 to be different from 3A.

b. Suppose a country's postal codes consist of three characters. A code may have three letters, three numbers, or a combination of letters and numbers. How many three-character codes are possible?

c. Suppose a country's postal codes have six characters that are a mixture of letters and numbers, such as CB2 1QA, 3B2 A3H, and V6J 1Z8. How many six-character codes are possible?

Note: For 15–18, you may want to give students population figures rather than having them research them. Many factors affect a state's actual ratio of possible plates to population. Some states use a different license-plate system for vehicles that are not passenger cars, such as trucks or commercial vehicles. Some states allow vehicle owners to continue using license plates from previous series, and some offer special plates with different letter-number combinations. Vanity plates may contain very different letter-number sequences. States' license-plate schemes change often; students may also want to research current schemes.

Extensions

14. The factors of 118 are 2 and 59. The number 59 is prime, with factors of 1 and 59. This means that there would have to be 2 suspects, 1 room, and 59 weapons, or some such combination, which is highly unlikely.

15. With a population of about 18,592,000 and $26^4 \times 10^3 = 456,976,000$ possible plates, the Texas ratio is $456,976,000 \div 18,592,000 \approx 24.6$.

16. With a population of about 9,575,000 and $26^3 \times 10^3 + 10^3 \times 26^3 = 17,576,000 + 17,576,000 = 35,152,000$ possible plates, the Michigan ratio is $35,152,000 \div 9,575,000 \approx 3.7$.

17. With a population of about 634,000 and $26^3 \times 10^3 = 17,576,000$ possible plates, the Alaska ratio is $17,576,000 \div 634,000 \approx 27.7$.

18. With a population of about 1,944,000 and $26^3 \times 10^3 = 17,576,000$ possible plates, the Utah ratio is $17,576,000 \div 1,944,000 \approx 9.0$

19. Note: These answers assume a 26-letter alphabet.

19a. $36^2 = 1296$ codes (There are 36 possibilities for each position.)

19b. $36^3 = 46,656$ codes

19c. $36^6 = 2,176,782,336$ codes

Mathematical Reflections

In this investigation, you developed strategies for counting in situations in which there are many possibilities. These questions will help you summarize what you have learned:

1 Suppose you are given a list of options in each of several categories. You are to choose one option from each category. Describe how you could make a counting tree to help you find all the possible combinations of options. Use an example if it helps you to explain your thinking.

2 Suppose you must choose one option from each of three categories. The first category has two options, the second has three options, and the third has three options. Describe how you could list all the possible combinations without using a counting tree. Use an example if it helps you to explain your thinking.

3 In counting situations in which there are many possibilities, making a counting tree or a list can be time-consuming and cumbersome. In these cases, you can do calculations to find the number of possibilities. Look back at your work in this investigation. Find an example of a counting problem you solved by doing calculations. Describe the problem, and explain the strategy you used to find your answer.

Think about your answers to these questions, discuss your ideas with other students and your teacher, and then write a summary of your findings in your journal.

Imagine that you are writing a mystery story about a detective's investigation of a crime. What type of crime would you write about? Describe some of the characters you might include. What situations could you include in your story that would require the detective to count possibilities? You will continue to brainstorm about your story at the end of each investigation.

Tips for the Linguistically Diverse Classroom

Original Rebus The Original Rebus technique is described in detail in *Getting to Know Connected Mathematics*. Students make a copy of the text before it is discussed. During the discussion, they generate their own rebuses for words they do not understand; the words are made comprehensible through pictures, objects, or demonstrations. Example: Question 3—Key words and phrases for which students might make rebuses are *counting tree* (sketch of one), *time-consuming* (1:00–6:00), *calculations* ($a \times b \times c$), *look back at your work* (list the pages related to this investigation).

TEACHING THE INVESTIGATION

1.1 • Making Faces

This problem opens with a description of the robbery that students will follow throughout the unit. Counting problems are built around the details of a detective's investigation. The situation in this problem—a police artist creating a sketch of a suspect—involves visual clues rather than numerical or alphabetical clues. Students will discover that with only a few possibilities for each feature, a great number of faces are possible. Students are encouraged to invent their own ways of analyzing the problem.

Launch

Introduce the context of the unit: the owner of an electronics store reports that compact disc players were stolen from his storage locker. A detective is called in to investigate. Review with the class the detective's initial findings.

Discuss the police artist's list of choices for possible features.

> How many choices are there for hair? *(2)* For eyes? *(4)* For a nose? *(4)*

> In this problem, you will explore how many possible facial descriptions can be made from these choices.

Since this is the first problem in the unit, students will need time to think about how they might count such possibilities. They may decide to draw pictures of the set of possibilities or to make a list using words or letters for the various choices. Observing the creation of several different combinations should give them an indication of the great number of combinations that are possible with only a few choices for each feature.

> Does the order in which the artist draws the features matter? *(no)*

> Must exactly one choice be made for each feature?

In this problem, one and only one attribute must be chosen for each feature.

Brainstorm with students about their beginning ideas about how many facial descriptions they think are possible. Ask for some ideas about how they might begin the problem.

Have students explore the problem and the follow-up individually or in pairs.

Explore

Encourage students to be systematic in their approach to the problem. If any students are having trouble, ask whether making an organized list or a counting tree that includes all the possible choices would be helpful. This is a reasonable strategy for part A. For part B, however, the number of choices becomes so great that making a complete counting tree is not very efficient. By looking at their counting trees for part A, students should begin to move toward using multiplication to count the number of combinations.

Consider asking some students to put their diagrams, lists, or other strategies on large sheets of paper to facilitate sharing later.

Here are two ways students might approach part A:

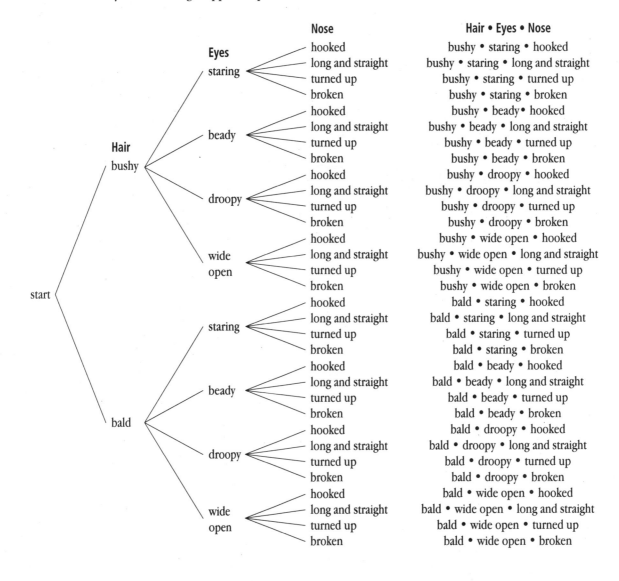

Summarize

Ask some students to share how they solved the problem and constructed their diagrams. If no one offers a counting tree as a solution method, suggest it yourself. While reviewing the construction of a counting tree, ask these questions:

What are the different features? What are the possible attributes for each feature?

How *many* choices are there for hair? For eyes? For a nose?

What mathematical operation is indicated by the number of choices in the counting tree? Can you see a shortcut for predicting how many possibilities the counting tree will show?

Suppose we eliminated a choice, such as deleting the "broken nose" attribute from the list of nose descriptions. How would that impact the total number of facial descriptions?

Which feature or features have the greatest impact on the total number of facial descriptions? In other words, to which feature or features would adding one more choice make the greatest difference: adding a new style of hair, or eyes, or nose, or mouth?

This may be hard for students to analyze. If they have discovered the multiplication method, the following analysis could be discussed: there are 2 (hair choices) × 4 (eye choices) × 4 (nose choices) × 3 (mouth choices), or 96 combinations. Adding one more hair choice would give 144 combinations. Adding one more eye choice or one more nose choice would give 120 combinations. Adding one more mouth choice would give 128 combinations. Thus, increasing the number of choices for the feature with the *fewest* choices has the greatest impact.

If a group made an organized list, they might see that the list contains patterns that show groups of possibilities, which again suggests multiplication as a shortcut.

You want students to begin to look for shortcuts, but the hands-on modeling is an important part of making sense of such problems, so don't push too hard for a formula or a counting principle. With additional investigations, students will find the need for a generalized way of counting possibilities more and more compelling.

1.2 • Checking Plate Numbers

States have different systems for issuing vehicle license plates. For example, some use a digit followed by three letters and three more numbers; some use three numbers followed by three letters. Some states need more combinations than others, and the number of combinations changes with the system. The number of choices for an individual element in a sequence depends on whether it can be a letter or a number. In this problem, students explore combinations of letters and numbers on license plates. They are encouraged to focus on effective strategies for modeling and determining the number of possible combinations.

Launch

To introduce the problem, bring in a license plate from your state, or draw one on the board.

How many choices are there for the first position? How many choices are there for the second position?

Students should realize that there are 26 choices for each letter and 10 choices for each number (assuming that all letters and numbers can be used). You may find the language of "filling in the slots" helpful for talking about these ideas with students.

Ask the following questions to start students thinking about the issues in this problem, though students are unlikely to have complete answers at this stage.

> How many choices do you think there are in all for the positions on this license plate?

> How could you make an argument to show that your answer is correct?

> How might this number relate to the number of people living in the state?

If students mention the fact that there are some number and letter combinations that states won't print on license plates, explain that in this problem they will assume that all combinations are possible.

Now refer to the problem facing the detective.

> Do you think the eyewitness report about the partly identified license plate will help the detective to identify the driver of the van?

Have students work on the problem and the follow-up in pairs.

Explore

To answer the question, students must find a way to determine how many license plates could start with the letters MTU. Again, if they have trouble getting started, suggest that they begin an organized list or a counting tree and look for patterns that would help them to compute the number of possibilities.

> There are far too many possibilities to list them all or to make a complete counting tree, but beginning one can help you think about the problem.

For students who are struggling, you might ask how many three-digit numbers there are (from 000 to 999) and how this relates to the problem.

Listen carefully to students' conversations so that you can call on students to present a range of ideas in the summary.

Summarize

Have students share how they reasoned about the problem. Following are three strategies they might suggest.

■ Some will recognize that the combination 000 is the least possible for three digits and that 999 is the greatest. There are exactly 1000 numbers in this list: 999 numbers from 001 to 999 plus the additional possibility of 000.

- Some may think about how many choices there are for each position:

10 choices	10 choices	10 choices

- Some may begin making lists, for example:

1	**0**	**?**

How many ways can this end?

1	**1**	**?**

How many ways can this end?

and so on . . .

If some students used a counting tree, ask them to explain how the diagram helped their thinking. (Counting trees can be useful, but not in every context.) Once students have shared their ideas, help them to see that multiplication is an appropriate solution strategy.

> Suppose that a less populated state issues license plates containing three letters followed by *two* numbers. How many license plates containing the sequence MTU would be possible?
>
> How does knowing that there are 10 choices for the first position and 10 choices for the second position help you to predict the number of possible plates?
>
> How many numbers are there from 0 to 99? How does this relate to the number of choices?

To assess whether students are focusing on how many choices there are for each decision that must be made, ask:

> How is the license-plate problem different from the facial-descriptions problem? *(In the first problem, the choices are the attributes for each feature; here they are the digits that can be in a particular place in a number. Also, the choices for each feature in the facial-descriptions problem are different; the possibilities for some positions in the license plate are the same.)*
>
> How is the license-plate problem similar to the facial-descriptions problem? *(In both problems, you can multiply the choices together to obtain the total number of possibilities.)*

Additional Answers

ACE Answers

Connections

2a. Possible answer: salad, orange juice, fruit; pizza, milk, frozen yogurt; pizza, orange juice, pie; turkey sandwich, milk, pudding

2b.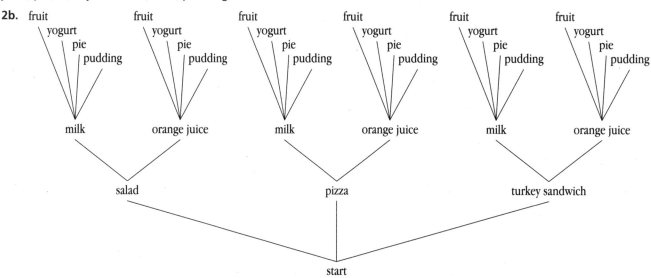

2c. 3 × 2 × 4 = 24 days

Mathematical Reflections

1. Suppose you are making a counting tree for a sequence of three categories with three options for the first category, two for the second, and two for the third. From the start position, draw branches to represent each of the three options for the first category, labeling each branch to show what option is represented. From the end of each first-category branch, draw and label branches for each of the two options in the second category. Finally, draw and label branches for each of the two options in the third category.

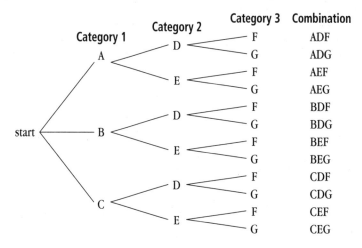

To find all the possible combinations of options, count the combinations at the end of the third-category branches.

2. You can name the options so that they are easy to refer to: first category (2 choices), A and B; second category (3 choices), L, M, and N; third category (3 choices), X, Y, and Z. When making a list, you have to be systematic so that you don't miss any combinations. One way to be systematic is to keep the first two choices the same until all possibilities beginning with those two choices have been listed. Then change the second choice and repeat the third choices. For example:

ALX	AMX	ANX	BLX	BMX	BNX
ALY	AMY	ANY	BLY	BMY	BNY
ALZ	AMZ	ANZ	BLZ	BMZ	BNZ

3. When you can't make a counting tree or a list, you can think about the number of possibilities for each category and picture the branches in your mind. For example, the state in which the robbery took place issues license plates with six characters, three letters followed by three numbers. To make a plate, you have to fill six positions. You have 26 choices for the first position. If you were making a counting tree, you would start with 26 branches. The second position has 26 options, so each of the 26 branches would have 26 branches coming from it—making $26 \times 26 = 676$ branches so far. The third position also has 26 options, for $676 \times 26 = 17{,}576$ branches. There are 10 options for the fourth position, so 10 branches would come from each of the 17,576 branches, a total of 175,760 branches. The fifth position adds 10 branches from each of these, a total of 1,757,600 branches. The sixth position adds 10 branches from each of these, a total of 17,576,000 ending branches. There are $26 \times 26 \times 26 \times 10 \times 10 \times 10 = 17{,}576{,}000$ possibilities.

Opening Locks

Much of the power of mathematics arises from the fact that ideas and procedures used in one situation can be applied in many others that may initially appear quite different. The key is uncovering the structural properties that make the situations mathematically similar. In this investigation, students become aware of some fundamental properties of counting that can be found in situations that, on the surface, may seem unrelated.

Systematically listing possibilities is a useful strategy for Problem 2.1, Pushing Buttons, in which students investigate the number of possible sequences for push-button locks. The counting of possible combinations can be expedited by multiplication. In Problem 2.2, Dialing Combinations, students explore the number of possible combinations for a combination lock. In Problem 2.3, Increasing Security, they analyze the relationship between the number of marks on a lock and the number of possible combinations.

One overall goal of the unit is to develop students' ability to recognize the structure of a problem that will involve some counting technique. Thus, it is important that students spend time thinking about the components of the problems and asking themselves what they need to know. To help them see useful connections among various multiplication problems, it will be important for you to focus their attention on similarities and differences among the situations. At several points in the investigation, ask students to think about how a problem is similar to and different from earlier problems. Also ask students to reflect on how the solution strategies they are using are similar and different.

Mathematical and Problem-Solving Goals

- *To further explore counting situations in which multiplication provides an answer*
- *To construct systematic lists of outcomes for complex processes*
- *To uncover patterns that help in counting the outcomes of complex processes*
- *To recognize that one problem has the same structure as another problem*

Materials		
Problem	For students	For the teacher
All	Graphing calculators	Transparencies: 2.1 to 2.3 (optional)
2.2		Combination lock (optional)

INVESTIGATION 2

Opening Locks

The manager of Fail-Safe suspects that the security guard stole Rodney's CD players. He suggested to Detective Curious that the guard had tried different combinations until the lock opened. The detective wondered how long it would take to try every possible combination.

2.1 Pushing Buttons

Some of the lockers at Fail-Safe have push-button locks that consist of five lettered buttons.

To open a push-button lock, the letters must be pressed in the correct sequence.

Problem 2.1

A lock sequence may have two, three, four, or five letters. A letter may not occur more than once in a sequence.

A. How many two-letter sequences are possible?

B. How many three-letter sequences are possible?

C. How many four-letter sequences are possible?

D. How many five-letter sequences are possible?

E. The security guard would not have known whether the sequence that would open Rodney's lock consisted of two, three, four, or five letters. How many possible lock sequences might she have had to try?

[handwritten notes in margins:]
Does order matter? yes
Can our repeat? no
Compare w/ facial prob.

Why are 4 letter + 5 letter seqs equal?
— all choices here are from same
— both use mult'n choices
— choices change as you use some up.
— order matters here
— items cannot repeat in either case.

Investigation 2: Opening Locks **15**

Answers to Problem 2.1

A. $5 \times 4 = 20$ possible sequences

B. $5 \times 4 \times 3 = 60$ possible sequences

C. $5 \times 4 \times 3 \times 2 = 120$ possible sequences

D. $5 \times 4 \times 3 \times 2 \times 1 = 120$ possible sequences

E. $20 + 60 + 120 + 120 = 320$ possible sequences

[handwritten notes:]
Compare w/ license plates — here digits may not repeat.
— Both use mult'n
— Order matters in both.

At a Glance

Grouping:
small groups

Launch

- Discuss how the Fail-Safe push-button lock works.

- Focus students on the task of counting the number of possible sequences for each code length.

- Have groups of two to four explore the problem and follow-up.

Explore

- Observe students' solution strategies.

- Ask students to share shortcuts they find.

Summarize

- Have students share their solution strategies.

- Talk about the similarity of the lock problem to the facial-description and license-plate problems.

Assignment Choices

ACE questions 1, 8–10, and unassigned choices from earlier problems

2.2

Dialing Combinations

Handwritten notes at top:
5 secs 320 = 1600 secs = 26.6 min.
10 sec 53⅓ min.
30 sec < 2 hrs

■ **Problem 2.1 Follow-Up** *omit.*

1. How long do you think it would take to try every possible lock sequence? Explain how you made your estimate.

2. Based on your work, do you think it is likely that someone opened Rodney's lock by trying all the possible lock sequences? Explain. *possibly*

3. Does your answer to question 2 make you suspicious of anyone who was near the crime scene? Explain.

2.1 FU

At a Glance

Grouping:
individuals, then pairs

Handwritten: *see back* **2.2 Dialing Combinations**

Handwritten margin:
2
120 . 5 = 600
120 . 4 = 40
60 . 3 = 180
20 . 2 = 40
————
1320 secs

The detective was trying to make her case based on the push-button lock data when she discovered that Rodney's locker has a *combination* lock!

Launch

■ Discuss how the Fail-Safe combination lock works.

■ Ask students to guess the combination of a particular lock. *(optional)*

■ Have students begin the problem individually and then complete the problem and do the follow-up in pairs.

The combination locks at Fail-Safe have combinations consisting of three numbers from 0 to 39 in a given order, such as 15-5-33 and 7-11-21. Do you think it would have been possible for someone to try every possible combination?

Explore

■ If students are struggling, help them develop a listing strategy.

Handwritten: Note: #5 cannot repeat.

Summarize

■ Ask students to explain their counting strategies.

■ Review a listing strategy with the class. *(optional)*

■ Discuss the follow-up questions.

> **Problem 2.2**
>
> **A.** How many possible combinations are there for Rodney's lock? Assume that a number may not appear more than once in a combination.
>
> **B.** How long do you think it would take someone to try all the possible combinations? Explain how you made your estimate.

Handwritten: Make lists for all possibilities for 2 digits / 3 digits
01 10 / 0 1 2 102
0 2 1 120

Assignment Choices

ACE questions 2–4, 11, 14, and unassigned choices from earlier problems

Answers to Problem 2.1 Follow-Up

See page 26h.

Answers to Problem 2.2

A. 40 × 39 × 38 = 59,280 possible combinations

B. Possible answer: Suppose it takes about 6 seconds to try a three-number combination. Using this estimate, it would take about 59,280 × 6 = 355,680 seconds, or 355,680 ÷ 60 = 5928 minutes, or 5928 ÷ 60 = 98.8 hours, or 98.8 ÷ 24 ≈ 4.12 days! Even if you could test a combination in 3 seconds, it would take more than 2 days to try them all. (Note: Students may raise the issue that the thief may be lucky enough to open the lock on the first try. Most will realize that the thief is not likely to have to try all the combinations, but there are so many possible combinations that even if the thief has an efficient method for keeping track of what has been tried and finds the correct combination halfway through, it would still take a very long time.)

omit – Use Pizza Prob instead.

■ Problem 2.2 Follow-Up

1. The detective started to list the possible lock combinations, but she soon became tired.

0-0-0	0-1-0	0-2-0
0-0-1	0-1-1	0-2-1
0-0-2	0-1-2	0-2-2
	0-1-3	
	0-1-4	
	0-1-5	
	0-1-6	
	0-1-8	
	0-1-9	

illustration disagrees w/ key

She then tried to make a counting tree, but she found it very tedious to draw. As she studied the patterns in her work, she had an idea:

"I can determine how many choices I have for each position in the combination. Then I can multiply those numbers together to predict the total number of possibilities!"

Do you think the detective's idea is reasonable? Why or why not?

2. For some locks, a combination may have the same number in the first and last positions but not in adjacent positions. This means that 3-1-3 is allowed, but 3-3-1 is not. If such combinations were allowed for the locks at Fail-Safe, how would the number of possible combinations for Rodney's lock change?

3. If you were in charge of security at Fail-Safe, would you recommend push-button locks or combination locks? Explain.

4. Does your work on this problem make you suspicious of anyone who was near the crime scene? Explain.

4·3·2 = 24 / 2 methods

4 digits

012   102   201   301
013   103   210   312
021   120   203   302
023   128   230   320
031   130   213   312
032   132   231   321

Answers to Problem 2.2 Follow-Up

1. The detective's method makes sense because if you drew a giant counting tree for the combinations, there would be 40 first branches, 39 branches off each of these, and 38 branches off each of *these*—a total of $40 \times 39 \times 38 = 59{,}280$ branches.

2. There are still 40 choices for the first digit and 39 choices for the second digit. For the third digit, the first number is also an option, so there are 39 choices. This is a total of $40 \times 39 \times 39 = 60{,}840$ possibilities, an increase of 1560 combinations.

3. Answers will vary. Most students will say combination locks are preferable because they have many more possible combinations than do push-button locks. Some will raise the issue of how easy it is to cut the shackle on a combination lock and may argue for a push-button lock with more letters.

4. See page 26h.

Increasing Security

At a Glance

Grouping:
small groups

Launch

- Review the number of combinations for locks with three and four marks.

- Have groups of two to four explore the problem and follow-up.

Explore

- Encourage groups to search for a pattern in their tables.

- Suggest that groups include multiplication calculations in their tables.

Summarize

- Have students explain their equations.

- Ask how the graph shows that the increase in combinations is not constant.

- Help the class explore the relationship that the graph represents.

In Problem 2.2, you found the number of possible combinations for a lock with 40 marks, representing the numbers from 0 to 39. Some combination locks have more or fewer than 40 marks. In this problem, you will explore the relationship between the number of marks on a lock and the number of possible combinations.

Problem 2.3

When the owner of Fail-Safe learned about the robbery, he told the manager to replace all the locks with more secure locks. However, he made it clear that he did not want to spend a lot of money. The manager did some research and found that combination locks with more marks are more expensive than locks with fewer marks. He wanted to convince the owner that the increased security provided by locks with more marks was worth the extra investment.

A. Make a table showing the number of possible combinations for locks with from 3 to 10 marks. Consider only three-number combinations with no repeated numbers. For example, to complete the row for 3 marks, consider all possible combinations of the numbers 0, 1, and 2.

Number of marks	Number of combinations
3	
4	
5	
6	
7	
8	
9	
10	

B. Use the pattern in your table to write an equation for the relationship between the number of marks, m, and the number of combinations, C.

C. Sketch a graph of your equation for m values from 3 to 10.

D. How could the manager use your graph to convince the owner to buy locks with more marks?

Assignment Choices

ACE questions 5–7, 12, 13, and unassigned choices from earlier problems

Assessment

It is appropriate to use the check-up after this problem.

Answers to Problem 2.3

A.

Number of marks	Number of combinations
3	$6 = 3 \times 2 \times 1$
4	$24 = 4 \times 3 \times 2$
5	$60 = 5 \times 4 \times 3$
6	$120 = 6 \times 5 \times 4$
7	$210 = 7 \times 6 \times 5$
8	$336 = 8 \times 7 \times 6$
9	$504 = 9 \times 8 \times 7$
10	$720 = 10 \times 9 \times 8$

B. $C = m(m - 1)(m - 2)$

C, D. See page 26h.

Problem 2.3 Follow-Up

1. Use your equation to find the number of possible combinations for Rodney's lock.

2. How does your answer to question 1 compare with the answer you would find by using the detective's strategy from Problem 2.2 Follow-Up?

3. **a.** If a lock has 40 marks and a combination consists of two numbers without repeats, how many combinations are possible? Explain your answer.

   b. If a lock has 40 marks and a combination consists of four numbers without repeats, how many combinations are possible? Explain your answer.

   c. If a lock has 20 marks and a combination consists of four numbers without repeats, how many combinations are possible? Explain your answer.

4. **a.** Suppose a combination consists of two numbers without repeats. Write an equation for the relationship between the number of marks, m, and the number of combinations, C.

   b. Suppose a combination consists of four numbers without repeats. Write an equation for the relationship between the number of marks, m, and the number of combinations, C.

Answers to Problem 2.3 Follow-Up

1. $C = m(m - 1)(m - 2) = 40(40 - 1)(40 - 2) = 40 \times 39 \times 38 = 59{,}280$ combinations

2. The answers are the same.

3. a. $C = 40 \times 39 = 1560$ combinations

   b. $C = 40 \times 39 \times 38 \times 37 = 2{,}193{,}360$ combinations

   c. $C = 20 \times 19 \times 18 \times 17 = 116{,}280$ combinations

4. a. $C = m(m - 1)$

   b. $C = m(m - 1)(m - 2)(m - 3)$

Answers

Applications

1a. 100,000 × 5 = 500,000 seconds

1b. 500,000 ÷ 60 ≈ 8333 minutes, 8333 ÷ 60 ≈ 139 hours, 139 ÷ 24 ≈ 5.8 days

1c. See below right.

1d. Possible answer: Lock designers could add more buttons to increase the number of combinations or design locks that shut down for a period of time if a certain number of incorrect sequences are entered in a row.

2a. 31 selections

2b. 31 selections

2c. 31 selections

2d. 31 selections

Applications • Connections • Extensions

As you work on these ACE questions, use your calculator whenever you need it.

Applications

1. Tina's new car has a push-button lock. The car is locked, and Tina has forgotten the lock sequence. She is trying to open the lock by testing each possible sequence. It takes her 5 seconds to test each sequence. The manufacturer says that there are 100,000 possible sequences.

   a. If Tina has to test every possible sequence, how many seconds will it take her to open the car door?

   b. Express your answer to part a in minutes, in hours, and in days.

   c. Make a table and a graph of the relationship between number of minutes and number of combinations tested.

   d. How could lock designers protect owners against people who might try to break into cars by trying possible lock sequences?

2. To play the Take-3 lottery game, players must choose three numbers from 0 to 30 in a particular order. The same number may appear more than once in a selection. The order of the numbers is considered, so 3-2-4 is different from 4-3-2. If a player's selection matches the winning selection, the player wins the grand prize.

   a. How many possible selections begin with 0-0?

   b. How many possible selections begin with 0-1?

   c. How many possible selections begin with 0-2?

   d. How many possible selections begin with 0-3?

1c. Tina can try 12 combinations every minute. The table shows some data that fit this relationship.

Minutes	Combinations tested
0	0
1	12
2	24
3	36
4	48
5	60
6	72
7	84
8	96

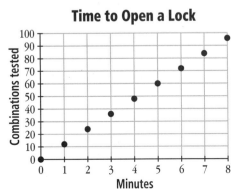

Time to Open a Lock

e. How many possible selections begin with 0?

f. What is the total number of possible selections?

g. Freija says that if she purchases a Take-3 lottery ticket every day for a year, she is guaranteed to win at least once. Do you agree? Explain.

h. If you could write one selection every 2 seconds, how long would it take you to list all the possibilities? Express your answer in seconds, in minutes, in hours, in days, and in weeks.

3. The Guess-and-Win lottery game requires players to choose three *different* numbers from 0 to 30. The order of the numbers matters, so 3-2-4 is different from 4-3-2.

a. How many possible selections begin with 0-1?

b. How many possible selections begin with 0-2?

c. How many possible selections begin with 0-3?

d. How many possible selections begin with 0?

e. How many possible selections begin with 1?

f. What is the total number of possible selections?

4. Which of the following has the greatest number of possible combinations? Explain how you arrived at your answer.

  i. a lock with 10 numbers for which a combination consists of 3 numbers with repeated numbers allowed

  ii. a lock with 5 numbers for which a combination consists of 5 numbers with repeated numbers allowed

  iii. a lock with 5 numbers for which a combination consists of 5 numbers with repeated numbers *not* allowed

2e. 31 × 31 = 961 selections

2f. 31 × 31 × 31 = 29,791 selections

2g. With 29,791 different three-number selections, it is not likely that any particular selection will win at least once in a year. In fact, each can be expected to be the winning selection once every 29,791 ÷ 365 ≈ 81.6 years!

2h. 29,791 × 2 = 59,582 seconds, 59,582 ÷ 60 ≈ 993 minutes, 993 ÷ 60 ≈ 16.55 hours, 16.55 ÷ 24 ≈ 0.69 day, 0.69 ÷ 7 ≈ 0.10 week (This assumes you take no breaks.)

3a. 29 selections (0 and 1 cannot be used in the last position.)

3b. 29 selections

3c. 29 selections

3d. 30 × 29 = 870 selections (0 cannot be used in the second position, so there are 30 choices for that position and 29 choices for the last position.)

3e. 30 × 29 = 870 selections

3f. 31 × 30 × 29 = 26,970 selections

4. Lock i has 10 × 10 × 10 = 1000 possible combinations, lock ii has 5 × 5 × 5 × 5 × 5 = 3125, and lock iii has 5 × 4 × 3 × 2 × 1 = 120, so lock ii has the greatest number of possible combinations.

5a. Possible answer: 3-1-8, 7-6-9, 0-0-7, 8-8-8, and 8-0-8

5b. There are 1000 possible combinations. The combinations range from 000 to 999, which is 1000 possibilities, or a total of $10^3 = 1000$ possibilities.

6a. Possible answer: 1-2-3-4-5, 4-8-9-1-0, 4-4-2-7-3, 5-5-5-5-5, and 7-5-3-5-7

6b. There are 100,000 possible combinations. The combinations range from 00000 to 99999, which is 100,000 possibilities, or a total of $10^5 = 100,000$ possibilities.

5. Some bicycle locks are composed of several numbered wheels. To open the lock, you line up the correct sequence of numbers with the arrow.

Suppose a bicycle lock has three wheels with the numbers from 0 to 9 on each wheel.

a. List five possible combinations for this lock.

b. How many possible combinations are there? Explain how you found your answer.

6. Suppose a bicycle lock has five wheels with the numbers from 0 to 9 on each wheel. To open the lock, you line up the correct sequence of numbers with the arrow.

a. List five possible combinations for this lock.

b. How many possible combinations are there? Explain how you found your answer.

7. Suppose a lock has three wheels with the numbers from 0 to 4 on each wheel. To open the lock, you line up the correct sequence of numbers with the arrow.

    a. List five possible combinations for this lock.

    b. How many possible combinations are there? Explain how you found your answer.

Connections

8. Sammy looks in his closet and sees four shirts, three pairs of jeans, high-top tennis shoes, running shoes, and three caps. He wants to wear a shirt, a pair of jeans, shoes, and a cap. How many different outfits can he make?

9. Winona and her friends walk to the pizza parlor for dinner. They decide to order the special, a cheese pizza with one topping and a choice of crust. The choices for toppings are onions, mushrooms, green peppers, olives, pepperoni, ham, and sausage. The choices for crust are garlic, sesame seed, whole wheat, and extra crispy. How many different pizzas are possible?

Tonight's Special

A large cheese pizza with one topping and choice of crust

$8.99

10. A lock has five buttons, labeled A, B, C, D, and E. A combination consists of five letters pressed in a particular order. A letter may be repeated. Some possible combinations are A-B-A-A-E and D-D-D-D-D. How many combinations are possible?

11. **a.** How many different eight-letter "words" can you make by rearranging the letters in the word COMPUTER? In this situation, a "word" is any combination that includes each letter in COMPUTER exactly once. Two possible words are TRPOCMEU and ETOUMPCR.

    b. Which lock problem does this resemble? Explain.

7a. Possible answer: 4-3-2, 0-1-4, 2-2-3, 1-1-1, and 3-0-3

7b. There are $5^3 = 125$ possible combinations.

Connections

8. $4 \times 3 \times 2 \times 3 = 72$ different outfits

9. $7 \times 4 = 28$ different pizzas

10. $5 \times 5 \times 5 \times 5 \times 5 = 3125$ combinations

11a. There are 8 choices for the first position, 7 for the second, 6 for the third, and so on, for a total of $8 \times 7 \times 6 \times 5 \times 4 \times 3 \times 2 \times 1 = 40,320$ words.

11b. Since we cannot have repeats, and since we are thinking of arrangements of letters, this resembles the push-button lock problem: making a word is equivalent to opening a lock by pressing each of 8 buttons once. This is also similar to a combination-lock problem in which the dial has 8 marks and the combination has 8 numbers, with no repeats.

12a. i. 4 code words: 0-0, 0-1, 1-0, and 1-1 (or 2^2 = 4 code words)

ii. 8 code words: 0-0-0, 0-0-1, 0-1-0, 0-1-1, 1-0-0, 1-0-1, 1-1-0, and 1-1-1 (or 2^3 = 8 code words)

iii. 2^4 = 16 code words

iv. 2^n code words

12b. See below right.

Extensions

13a. The ten-wheel lock has more combinations than the five-wheel lock—almost 100 times as many.

i. 10^5 = 100,000 combinations

ii. 5^{10} = 9,765,625 combinations

13b. n^5 and 5^n are equal when $n = 5$. When $n > 5$, $5^n > n^5$. When $n = 2, 3,$ or 4, $n^5 > 5^n$. When $n = 1$, $5^n > n^5$.

i. The lock with 5 wheels has n^5 combinations.

ii. The lock with n wheels has 5^n combinations.

---

12. Randy is helping his little sisters develop a secret code for their club. The girls want their code words to be made up of combinations of 0s and 1s, and they want to make a list of messages that correspond to the code words. For example, 01 might mean "meet me after school," and 010 might mean "bring your bike."

a.   **i.**   How many two-digit code words are possible?

      ii.   How many three-digit code words are possible?

      iii.   How many four-digit code words are possible?

      iv.   How many n-digit code words are possible?

b.   Make a table and a graph and write an equation to show the relationship between the length of a code word and the number of possible code words. What kind of relationship does your graph reveal?

Extensions

13. a.   Find the number of possible combinations for each lock described, and tell how the two numbers compare.

      i.   a bicycle lock composed of five wheels with ten numbers on each wheel

      ii.   a bicycle lock composed of ten wheels with five numbers on each wheel

b.   Find the number of possible combinations for each lock described, and tell how the two numbers compare.

      i.   a bicycle lock composed of five wheels with n numbers on each wheel

      ii.   a bicycle lock composed of n wheels with five numbers on each wheel

24   **Clever Counting**

12b. $C = 2^n$, where C is the number of code words; This is an exponential relationship.

Length of code word	Number of code words
1	2
2	4
3	8
4	16
n	2^n

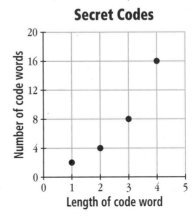

Secret Codes

24   **Investigation 2**

14. In the Take-Your-Chances lottery game, players choose three numbers from 0 to 30 in a particular order. A number may appear more than once in a selection. To win the grand prize, a player must have selected the winning numbers in the correct order. A player wins a smaller prize if he or she has selected the winning numbers but in an incorrect order.

    a. Suppose this week's winning selection is 8-13-21. List all the selections for which a prize will be awarded.

    b. Suppose this week's winning selection is 9-18-27. List all the selections for which a prize will be awarded.

    c. If a player makes one selection for next week's game, what is the probability that he or she will win the grand prize? What is the probability that he or she will win a smaller prize?

    d. Let a, b, and c represent any three numbers. In how many different orders can a, b, and c be written?

Did you know?

You can use the *factorial* function on your calculator to help you solve problems about combinations. The factorial symbol is an exclamation point. When an exclamation point appears after a whole number, it means "multiply all the whole numbers up to and including this number." For example, 6! represents $1 \times 2 \times 3 \times 4 \times 5 \times 6$.

The number of possible four-number combinations with no repeats that you can make from four numbers is $4 \times 3 \times 2 \times 1$. You can evaluate this by entering 4! on your calculator. What problem can you solve by entering 5! on your calculator?

14a. grand prize: 8-13-21; smaller prize: 8-21-13, 13-8-21, 13-21-8, 21-8-13, 21-13-8

14b. grand prize: 9-18-27; smaller prize: 9-27-18, 18-9-27, 18-27-9, 27-9-18, 27-18-9

14c. Repeats are allowed, so there are $31^3 = 29{,}791$ combinations. Only one will win the grand prize, a probability of $\frac{1}{29{,}791} \approx 0.00003$. Five will win a smaller prize, a probability of $\frac{5}{29{,}791} \approx 0.00017$.

14d. There are six ways to write the letters: *abc, acb, bac, bca, cab,* and *cba.*

Tips for the Linguistically Diverse Classroom

Rebus Scenario The Rebus Scenario technique is described in detail in *Getting to Know Connected Mathematics.* This technique involves sketching rebuses on the chalkboard that correspond to key words in the story or information that you present orally. Example: Some key phrases for which you may need to draw rebuses while discussing the "Did you know?" feature: *exclamation point* (!), *whole numbers* (5, 6, 7, . . .).

Possible Answers

1. $5 \times 4 \times 3 = 60$ combinations

2. $n(n-1)(n-2)$ combinations

3. $n(n-1)(n-2)(n-3)$ $\cdots (n-r)$ combinations

4. The two problems are basically the same. The multiplication strategy will work in each case; you just have to know how many choices you have to start with. To make sure that you have no repeats, you reduce the number of choices by 1 for each new position in the combination. For the combination lock that allows the first and third positions to be the same number, you add 1 to the choices in the third position.

Mathematical Reflections

In this investigation, you learned strategies for finding the number of possible combinations for push-button locks and combination locks. These questions will help you summarize what you have learned:

1. Suppose a lock has five numbers. How many three-number combinations are possible if repeated numbers are not allowed?

2. Suppose a lock has n numbers. How many three-number combinations are possible if repeated numbers are not allowed? Assume $n \geq 3$.

3. Suppose a lock has n numbers. How many r-number combinations are possible if repeated numbers are not allowed? Assume $n \geq r$.

4. Compare the strategies you used to find the number of possible sequences for push-button locks with the strategies you used to find the number of combinations for combination locks. Consider two types of combination locks:

- locks for which combinations with repeated numbers are not allowed

- locks for which the first and third numbers of the combination may be the same

Think about your answers to these questions, discuss your ideas with other students and your teacher, and then write a summary of your findings in your journal.

What situations might you include in your mystery story that would require the detective to estimate how long it would take to do or make something?

Tips for the Linguistically Diverse Classroom

Original Rebus The Original Rebus technique is described in detail in *Getting to Know Connected Mathematics*. Students make a copy of the text before it is discussed. During the discussion, they generate their own rebuses for words they do not understand; the words are made comprehensible through pictures, objects, or demonstrations. Example: Question 1—Key phrases for which students might make rebuses are *lock has five numbers* (sketch of one), *three-number combinations* (2-4-5), *repeated numbers are not allowed* (5-3-3).

TEACHING THE INVESTIGATION

2.1 • Pushing Buttons

In this problem, students explore the number of possible combinations for a push-button lock consisting of five lettered buttons. In these locks, letters may not be repeated within a code. Despite the superficial differences between this problem and those students have previously encountered, the structure of this problem in terms of counting possibilities is identical to the facial-descriptions and license-plate problems: students must enumerate the number of choices for each position in the code and then determine the appropriate operation for computing the total number of possible codes.

Launch

Talk about how the push-button lock that is described in the student edition works: when the correct combination of letters is pressed, the lock opens. Combinations may consist of from two to five letters, and a letter may not be repeated within a sequence.

Some students may relate experiences they have had with these kinds of locks. To interest them in the task, you might ask:

> Does the fact that the lock combinations can be of different lengths increase security?

Focus students on the task of counting the number of possible combinations, or sequences of letters, for codes of various lengths. Have them work in groups of two to four on the problem and the follow-up.

Explore

As students make organized lists or counting trees or invent other ways of counting the possible sequences, observe whether they find it necessary to actually make complete lists or whether they have developed ways to organize their thoughts efficiently. Encourage them to explain to each other any shortcuts they have discovered. The language they develop for talking about the choices for each position and the number of positions in each sequence will be helpful for making generalizations about these kinds of problems later.

For the follow-up, you might suggest that students try timing how long it would take to open a mock lock, including the time it takes to see whether the lock will open.

Summarize

Ask students to share their ideas for solving the problem. If they made lists, ask how they organized the lists and found the number of possible sequences. Help students move toward using multiplication by connecting the number of choices for each position to how they organized their lists.

After determining the number of possible sequences for each length code, ask students to compare the structure of this problem with the structure of those they explored in Investigation 1.

> How is this problem similar to the problem involving facial descriptions? How is it different? What are the components of each problem? What processes are involved in solving the problems?

> How is this problem similar to the problem involving license plates? How is it different? What are the components of each problem? What processes are involved in solving the problems?

As with the facial-descriptions and license-plate problems, this problem requires finding the number of choices that are possible for each position. It is different from the license-plate problem because repeated numbers are not allowed. It is different from the facial-descriptions problem because each position is being filled from the same set of elements. Also, in this and the license-plate problems, order is important; order is not an issue in the facial-descriptions problem.

2.2 • Dialing Combinations

Students have probably used combination locks, but they may never have considered how many possible combinations there are. This question is deliberately left open initially to encourage students to think about the factors in the problem and to ask themselves what they know and what they need to know. The follow-up offers some structure to this search.

Launch

The detective discovers that Rodney's locker has a combination lock. To open it, the correct combination consisting of three numbers from 0 to 39 must be used.

Make sure students know how combination locks are opened. Usually, the dial is turned clockwise several times and then stopped at the first number of the combination. The dial is next turned counterclockwise past the first number of the combination and then stopped at the second number of the combination. After a turn clockwise to the third number, the lock will open. There are other kinds of combination locks, but this problem assumes a three-number combination. Locks of this sort actually allow the same number in the first and third positions, but the problem has been simplified by not allowing repeats.

You might display a combination lock of your own and challenge students to guess its combination. After students make a few guesses, offer a clue.

> The first number is ___ . Does this help you?

A few unsuccessful guesses may help more students access the problem. Don't take this introductory discussion too far, though; you want students to concentrate on the structure of the problem and on the important factors rather than on finding a particular combination.

> Is it possible for the guard or her friend to have tried all the possible combinations?

Have students start the problem individually and then gather in pairs to share ideas, complete the problem, and do the follow-up.

Explore

Having students begin the problem individually will ensure that everyone has a chance to reason about what the problem is before someone else offers specific solutions. When everyone has had some time to think about the problem, have students confer with partners.

Students should consider two problems: (1) how to find the number of combinations and (2) how to estimate the amount of time it would take to try all of them. Coax students who arrive at a time estimate quickly to explain how they derived their estimate.

> On what does your time estimate depend?

> How do you know how many possible combinations there are?

Ask pairs of students whose estimates disagree wildly to compare their reasoning. If some students say it is not possible to make an estimate, ask what else they would need to know in order to do so, or ask them to confer with students who have reached an estimate.

Here are some ideas for listing strategies that may help students who are struggling.

■ One way to approach a counting problem is to begin an organized list of examples of the things to be counted—in this case, lock combinations. It also helps to consider a simple case first. For example, first list all possible combinations for a lock with only *three numbers*—0, 1, and 2. Find all possible *three-number* combinations with no repeats.

0-1-2	1-0-2	2-0-1
0-2-1	1-2-0	2-1-0

Next list all possible combinations for a lock with only *four numbers*—0, 1, 2, and 3. Again, find all possible *three-number* combinations with no repeats.

0-1-2	1-0-2	2-0-1	3-0-1
0-1-3	1-0-3	2-0-3	3-0-2
0-2-1	1-2-0	2-1-0	3-1-0
0-2-3	1-2-3	2-1-3	3-1-2
0-3-1	1-3-0	2-3-0	3-2-0
0-3-2	1-3-2	2-3-1	3-2-1

Look for a pattern in the results. For example, there are 6 combinations that begin with each of the digits 0, 1, 2, and 3, for a total of 24. Also, there are 4 choices for the first position in the combination, 3 for the second position, and 2 for the third position; and $4 \times 3 \times 2 = 24$.

■ Consider again the problem of counting combinations for Rodney's lock, which has 40 marks on the dial for the numbers 0, 1, 2, . . . , 39. Begin organized lists of the possible combinations for each starting digit.

0-1-2	0-2-1	0-3-1	0-4-1	0-5-1	0-6-1	0-7-1	$\cdots$
0-1-3	0-2-3	0-3-2	0-4-2	0-5-2	0-6-2	0-7-2	$\cdots$
0-1-4	0-2-4	0-3-4	0-4-3	0-5-3	0-6-3	0-7-3	$\cdots$
0-1-5	0-2-5	0-3-5	0-4-5	0-5-4	0-6-4	0-7-4	$\cdots$
0-1-6	0-2-6	0-3-6	0-4-6	0-5-6	0-6-5	0-7-5	$\cdots$
$\vdots$	$\vdots$	$\vdots$	$\vdots$	$\vdots$	$\vdots$	$\vdots$	

■ Look for patterns in the lists to help answer the questions that follow.

– What strategy is being used to write the lists in a systematic way so that all possibilities are represented? *(The first two digits are fixed; the last digit cycles through all 38 remaining possibilities.)*

– How many combinations will start with 0-1? *(38)* How many combinations will start with 0-2? *(38)* How many combinations will start with 0-3? *(38)*

– How many combinations will start with 0? *(39 × 38)*

– So, how many lock combinations are possible? *(40 × 39 × 38)*

Summarize

From the discussions you have heard, select a few students to report their conclusions. The discussion here can set the tone for the rest of the unit.

> Are the combinations countable? That is, is there a *finite number* of combinations?

You may want to discuss the listing strategies suggested in the "Explore" section with the whole class. Ask students what patterns they notice in the lists and how they might use these to predict further answers.

What does the number of combinations depend on? *(the number of marks on the dial and the number of positions in the combination)*

What does the estimated time depend on? *(how long it takes to try a combination and how many possible combinations there are)*

Are you are surprised by the number of possible combinations? Is this number greater than you would have guessed? Why is this number so great?

The multiplicative nature of the process should by now be emerging. Students are not expected to have discovered a formula for the pattern, but they should be able to use the construction of the lists to talk about the process.

Part B asks students to reason from the number of possible combinations.

What else do we need to know to estimate the amount of time it would take to try each combination?

Can we say exactly how long it will take to find the right combination, or can we only estimate the time by using probabilities?

If you have a combination lock, let students simulate opening the lock in order to estimate the time it takes to try a combination. Encourage them to try several numbers and average the time to obtain a better estimate.

Have some groups explain how they estimated the time it would take to try all the combinations. Discuss the follow-up questions, which will help students strengthen their understanding of the connection between multiplication and counting. Give students a chance to debate how their new information makes some of the possible suspects look more suspicious and others less so.

2.3 • Increasing Security

In this problem, students work with the familiar concept of rate of change as they analyze how the number of lock combinations increases as the number of marks on the dial increases. The relationship between the number of marks and the number of combinations is cubic, a relationship students briefly encountered in the unit *Frogs, Fleas, and Painted Cubes.*

Launch

Introduce the context of this problem: the manager is attempting to convince the owner to purchase combination locks with more marks because of the increased security they offer.

Review with the class the number of possible combinations for locks with three marks (representing the numbers 0, 1, and 2) and four marks (representing the numbers 0, 1, 2, and 3). You may want to list all the possible combinations to reinforce what students have discovered about the connection between the number of choices and multiplication.

Lock with 3 marks: 0, 1, and 2

$3 \times 2 \times 1 = 6$ combinations

0-1-2	
0-2-1	
1-0-2	
1-2-0	
2-0-1	
2-1-0	

Lock with 4 marks: 0, 1, 2, and 3

$4 \times 3 \times 2 = 24$ combinations

0-1-2	1-0-2	2-0-1	3-0-1
0-1-3	1-0-3	2-0-3	3-0-2
0-2-1	1-2-0	2-1-0	3-1-0
0-2-3	1-2-3	2-1-3	3-1-2
0-3-1	1-3-0	2-3-0	3-2-0
0-3-2	1-3-2	2-3-1	3-2-1

Ask:

> How does the number of combinations grow as the number of marks on the dial increases?

Allow a few minutes for students to talk about this idea, giving them a chance to recall the concept of rate of growth and the vocabulary they have acquired in previous units, such as *growth factor, constant growth, exponential growth, quadratic relationship,* and *cubic relationship.*

> The manager must make a recommendation to the owner about what type of combination lock to buy. The owner wants increased security, but he does not want to waste money. Your job is to help the manager make his case for purchasing locks with more marks.

Have students work in groups of two to four on the problem and the follow-up.

Explore

As students work in their groups to construct the table, encourage them to search for a pattern in the growth of the number of combinations. Suggest that they include in their tables the multiplication calculations that give the number of combinations. Seeing the multiplication makes the underlying equation, $C = m(m - 1)(m - 2)$, more apparent. Graphing calculators may be helpful for testing equations. Be sure students address part D, which asks how the manager could make the case for buying locks with more marks.

If a group is having difficulty, suggest that they test the pattern they have found and the related equations on locks with only a few marks. They can list all possible combinations for each number of marks until they are convinced that multiplication will always produce the correct answer.

In the follow-up questions, students strengthen their understanding of using multiplication to solve counting problems.

Summarize

Have students share and explain their equations. Help them relate the multiplication rule to things they have done that make sense to them.

> How does your equation relate to making a list of all possible combinations for a given lock?

If some students used the idea of counting trees to think about the number of possibilities, you might ask them to explain their reasoning to the class.

Be sure students agree on the equation. Give them a chance to graph the equation if they have not already done so.

> From evidence in the table or the graph, how can we tell that the number of combinations is not growing at a constant rate? *(The increase in the number of combinations is not constant for a constant increase in the number of marks.)*

> Do all the points along the graph make sense in terms of the situation?

Help students understand that only whole-number values of m make sense, but that seeing the continuous graph helps us to see the relationship.

> How can the manager use the information in the graph to convince the owner to buy locks with more marks? *(The table and the graph clearly show that the number of combinations is growing at an increasing rate. The manager can use the graph to convince the owner that as the number of marks on the dial increases, the number of possible combinations grows more rapidly—and more combinations means increased security.)*

> Look at your graph. What kind of relationship do you think this is?

Students will probably say that the graph looks exponential or quadratic. If so, have them change the window to display the graph in all four quadrants—perhaps with window settings of ⁻10 to 10 for the *x*-axis and ⁻800 to 800 for the *y*-axis. The graphs below show the equation graphed in just the first quadrant and then in all four quadrants.

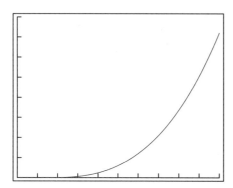 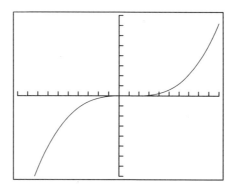

> Does this look like an exponential relationship now? Does it look like a quadratic relationship?

Students should realize that the equation is neither exponential nor quadratic; some may say it resembles the cubic relationships they saw in *Frogs, Fleas, and Painted Cubes.* Students will work more with cubic relationships in high school.

Additional Answers

Answers to Problem 2.1 Follow-Up

1. Possible answer: Suppose it takes 2 seconds to try a two-letter code, 3 seconds to try a three-letter code, 4 seconds to try a four-letter code, and 5 seconds to try a five-letter code. Based on these estimates, it would take about $(20 \times 2) + (60 \times 3) + (120 \times 4) + (120 \times 5) = 1300$ seconds, or about 22 minutes.

2. It seems possible that someone could open the lock by trying all the possible codes, assuming that person had an efficient method for keeping track of which codes had been tried. Also, it is likely that the lock would open before the last code had been tried.

3. The guard would have had enough time to test all the combinations when she was on patrol. And someone who had sneaked into the warehouse might have had time between the guard's rounds to open the lock by trial and error.

Answers to Problem 2.2 Follow-Up

4. Answers will vary. Many students will be suspicious of the manager because it seems unlikely that the guard could stumble on the lock combination in the time she had. The manager has the list of combinations. This does not prove anything, but the evidence seems to favor the guard's innocence.

Answers to Problem 2.3

C.

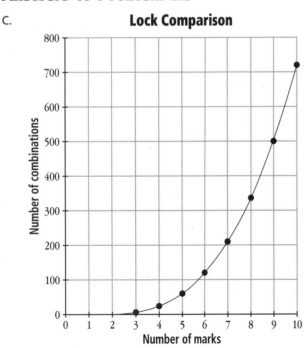

Lock Comparison

Number of combinations vs. *Number of marks*

D. The number of combinations grows at an increasing rate with a steady increase in the number of marks. The manager could explain to the owner that increasing the number of combinations would make it much more difficult for someone to break the code. He could use the graph to demonstrate the great increase in the number of combinations that results from each increase of 1 in the number of marks.

Networks

This investigation familiarizes students with a common counting application: finding the number of paths through a network. Networks offer visual representations of the multiplication technique, which can be applied to many other multistep processes. The basic idea of counting paths is that the number of ways to travel from point A to point C via point B is the product of the number of paths from A to B and the number of paths from B to C.

Problem 3.1, Making Rounds, introduces the idea of counting paths through a network in the context of the layout of the storage warehouse. In Problem 3.2, Networking, students explore network diagrams. The words *network, node,* and *edge* are introduced to make it easier for students to communicate about such diagrams. The question being asked is the same: How many paths are there from A to C through B? In Problem 3.3, Designing Networks, students are given constraints on the numbers of nodes and edges in a network and are asked to create networks that satisfy those constraints.

Mathematical and Problem-Solving Goals

- *To explore network applications*

- *To analyze the number of paths in a network*

- *To compare the structures of networks and problems involving combinations*

- *To create networks that satisfy given constraints*

Materials		
Problem	For students	For the teacher
All	Graphing calculators	Transparencies: 3.1A to 3.3B (optional), overhead graphing calculator (optional)
3.2	Large sheets of paper (optional)	

Networks

Detective Curious decided to investigate the possibility that someone broke into the ware-house while the night guard was on duty. The guard told the detective that, although she makes frequent rounds of the warehouse to inspect the locks and doors, she does not pass every locker on every trip through the warehouse. The detective thought the thief may have hidden in Rodney's locker during the guard's rounds. If the guard did not pass Rodney's locker, she would not have noticed that the lock had been opened.

3.1 Making Rounds

The floor plan of the Fail-Safe storage warehouse is shown below. The left section contains rows of small lockers, and the right section contains rows of large lockers. During each of her inspection rounds, the guard starts at checkpoint A and walks down an aisle of small lockers to checkpoint B. From there, she walks down an aisle of large lockers to checkpoint C. One possible path is shown in the diagram.

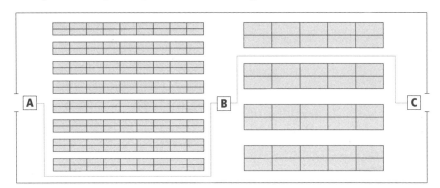

At a Glance

Grouping:
individuals or pairs

Launch

■ Help students familiarize themselves with the warehouse floor plan.

■ Have students work individually or in pairs on the problem and follow-up.

Explore

■ Suggest that students having trouble label the paths and begin an organized list.

■ Ask students to explain parallels between this problem and earlier problems.

Summarize

■ Have students share their solutions and strategies.

■ Help the class summarize connections between this and earlier problems.

Assignment Choices

ACE question 1 and unassigned choices from earlier problems

3.2

Networking

Grouping:
pairs

Launch

- Discuss a network diagram, including nodes, edges, and the paths through the network.

- Have pairs work on the problem and follow-up.

Explore

- Have some students put their work on large sheets of paper for sharing later. *(optional)*

Summarize

- Discuss the problem.

- Discuss the connections between the network problems and earlier counting problems.

- Talk about calculating round trips.

Problem 3.1

A. How many paths are there from A to B? How many paths are there from B to C?

B. How many paths are there from A to C through B? Explain your reasoning.

C. If Rodney has a small locker, how many of the paths from A to C pass by his locker?

D. If Rodney has a large locker, how many of the paths from A to C pass by his locker?

E. If Rodney has a small locker, what is the probability that the guard will *not* pass his locker on one of her rounds?

F. If Rodney has a large locker, what is the probability that the guard will *not* pass his locker on one of her rounds?

■ **Problem 3.1 Follow-Up**

1. Suppose the warehouse were laid out so that there were 15 paths from A to B and 12 paths from B to C. How would your answers to parts B–F of Problem 3.1 change?

2. Compare the method you used to count paths through the warehouse with the methods you used in previous investigations to count facial descriptions, license plates, and lock combinations.

(3.2) **Networking**

The diagram below is a model of the floor plan of the warehouse. A diagram like this is called a **network**. A network is made up of *nodes* and *edges*. In the network below, the nodes A, B, and C represent the warehouse checkpoints, and the edges connecting the nodes represent aisles between the rows of lockers. A *path* from node A to node C consists of an edge from node A to node B followed by an edge from node B to node C.

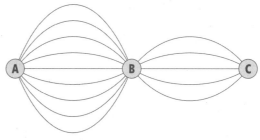

This network models the warehouse floor plan because it contains all the important information in a simplified form.

Assignment Choices

ACE questions 3, 4, 9, 10, and unassigned choices from earlier problems

Answers to Problem 3.1

A. There are nine paths from A to B and five paths from B to C.

B. There are $9 \times 5 = 45$ paths from A to C through B.

C. Only one path from A to B will pass by his locker if it is small; the path from B to C can be any of five possibilities. So, $1 \times 5 = 5$ of the 45 paths would pass by his locker.

D. Only one path from B to C will pass by his locker if it is large; the path from A to B can be any of nine possibilities. So, $9 \times 1 = 9$ of the 45 paths would pass by his locker.

E. The probability is $\frac{40}{45} \approx 0.89 \approx 89\%$.

F. The probability is $\frac{36}{45} = 0.8 = 80\%$.

Answers to Problem 3.1 Follow-Up

See page 36g.

Problem 3.2

A. In this network, a single edge connects node A to node B, and 8 edges connect node B to node C. How many paths are there from node A to node C that pass through node B?

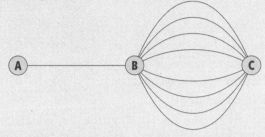

B. In this network, 2 edges connect node A to node B, and 5 edges connect node B to node C. How many paths are there from node A to node C that pass through node B?

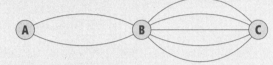

C. In another network, 25 edges connect node A to node B, and 32 edges connect node B to node C. How many paths are there from node A to node C that pass through node B? Explain your reasoning.

■ Problem 3.2 Follow-Up

1. For each network in Problem 3.2, find the number of different *round trips* from node A to node C and back to node A.

2. For parts A and B of Problem 3.2, describe how adding another edge connecting nodes A and B would change the number of round trips.

Answers to Problem 3.2

A. $1 \times 8 = 8$ paths

B. $2 \times 5 = 10$ paths

C. For each edge that connects nodes A and B, there are 32 ways to complete the path to node C, for a total of $25 \times 32 = 800$ paths.

Answers to Problem 3.2 Follow-Up

1. In part A, there are $1 \times 8 \times 8 \times 1 = 64$ round trips; in part B, there are $2 \times 5 \times 5 \times 2 = 100$ round trips; in part C, there are $25 \times 32 \times 32 \times 25 = 640,000$ round trips.

2. In part A, adding an edge would increase the number of rounds trips to $2 \times 8 \times 8 \times 2 = 256$, which is 4 times the number of round trips in the original network. Adding an edge in part B would increase the number of rounds trips to $3 \times 5 \times 5 \times 3 = 225$, which is 2.25 times the number of round trips in the original network.

Designing Networks

At a Glance

Grouping:
individuals, then pairs

Launch

- Read through part A as a class.

- Have students begin part A individually.

Explore

- Have pairs find the maximal network and then repeat the process for part B.

- Help students who are having trouble to draw one network that fits the conditions.

- Have pairs work on the follow-up.

Summarize

- Draw the networks for part A, and make a table of the data.

- Help students develop the equation relating the edges from A to B and the number of paths.

- Review parts B–D and the follow-up.

3.3 Designing Networks

You have found the number of paths through several networks. In this problem, you will design networks that satisfy given constraints.

Problem 3.3

A. 1. Design at least three networks with nodes A, B, and C and 12 edges. Each edge should connect node A to node B or node B to node C.

2. For each network you drew, record the number of edges from node A to node B, the number of edges from node B to node C, and the total number of paths from node A to node C. Look for a pattern in your results.

3. Use your findings from part 2 to help you draw the network with the maximum number of paths from node A to node C. Explain how you know that your network has the maximum number of paths.

B. Design a network with nodes A, B, C, and D and 12 edges that has the maximum number of paths from node A to node D through nodes B and C. How did you decide how to distribute the 12 edges?

C. Suppose you are given a specific number of nodes and a specific number of edges. How can you design a network with the maximum number of paths from the first node to the last node?

D. Describe how the numbers of edges between consecutive pairs of nodes are related to the total number of paths in a network.

■ Problem 3.3 Follow-Up

1. In the network below, how many paths are there from node A to node F?

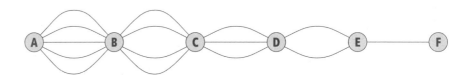

Assignment Choices

ACE questions 2, 5–8, and unassigned choices from earlier problems

Answers to Problem 3.3

A, B. See page 36g.

C. To produce the network with the maximum number of paths, distribute the edges equally, or as close to equally as possible, among the pairs of consecutive nodes.

D. The number of paths in a network is the product of the number of edges between all pairs of consecutive nodes.

2. In the network below, the number on each edge represents the time, in seconds, it takes to travel along that edge. Which path from node A to node F will take the least amount of time to travel? Explain your answer.

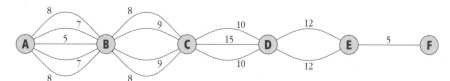

Answers to Problem 3.3 Follow-Up

1. $5 \times 4 \times 3 \times 2 \times 1 = 120$ paths

2. Choosing the "shortest" edge between each node gives a travel time of $5 + 8 + 10 + 12 + 5 = 40$ seconds.

Answers

Applications

1a. $2 \times 5 \times 3 = 30$ paths

1b. Six paths ($2 \times 1 \times 3$) pass the marked location.

2. See below right.

3. See page 36g.

4. See page 36h.

5. See below right.

6. See page 36h.

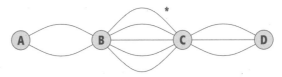

As you work on these ACE questions, use your calculator whenever you need it.

Applications

1. a. In the diagram below, how many paths are there from A to D?

b. How many paths from A to D pass the location represented by the asterisk?

2. Design a network with 3 nodes, 11 edges, and the maximum number of paths from the first node to the last node.

3. Design a network with nodes A, B, and C and exactly 12 paths from node A to node C that pass through node B.

4. Design a network with nodes A, B, and C and exactly 11 paths from node A to node C that pass through node B.

5. If possible, design a network with nodes A, B, C, and D and exactly 6 paths from node A to node D that pass through nodes B and C. If you think this cannot be done, explain why.

6. If possible, design a network with nodes A, B, C, and D and exactly 5 paths from node A to node D that pass through nodes B and C. If you think this cannot be done, explain why.

2. There are $5 \times 6 = 30$ paths in this network.

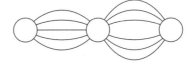

5. Possible answers (variations on these would work as well):

Connections

7. Shelly wants to build a rectangular pen for her dog Sam. She has 24 meters of fencing.

    a. Draw and label some rectangles that Shelly could form with the fencing.

    b. What are the dimensions of the rectangle that would give Sam the greatest area in which to run?

    c. How is this problem similar to part A of Problem 3.3?

8. In question 7, you explored rectangles that could be constructed from 24 meters of fencing.

    a. Write an equation for the relationship between the length of one side of the rectangle and the area enclosed by the fencing.

    b. Make a graph of the relationship between the length of one side of the rectangle and the area enclosed by the fencing.

    c. What type of relationship do your graph and table represent? Explain how you know.

Investigation 3: Networks 33

Connections

7. Note: This problem should look familiar to students. Half the perimeter is 12 meters, so the focus is on combinations that add to 12.

7a. See below left.

7b. A square with a side length of 6 m would give Sam the greatest area.

7c. In Problem 3.3, the number of edges from A to B and the number of edges from B to C add to 12; in this problem, the length and the width of the pen add to 12. In that problem, the maximum number of paths is achieved when the number of edges from A to B equals the number of edges from B to C; in this problem, the maximum area is achieved when the length equals the width.

8a. $A = l(12 - l)$, where A is the area enclosed by the fencing and l is the length of one side (Note: The perimeter is 24, so the width and the length add to 12. Thus the dimensions of the rectangle are l and $12 - l$. Students wrote identical equations in the unit *Frogs, Fleas, and Painted Cubes*.)

8b. See left.

8c. The relationship is quadratic because the graph is a parabola and the equation is the product of linear terms.

7a. Possible answer:

10 m / 2 m

9 m / 3 m

7.5 m / 4.5 m

8b.
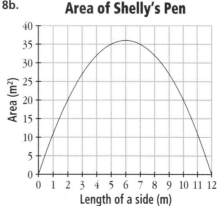

Area of Shelly's Pen

Investigation 3 33

9a. Possible answer: EEESSS, SSSEEE, ESSEES, ESESES, SESESE (Any combination of 3 E's and 3 S's will work.)

9b. See page 36h.

9c. 60

10a. See below right.

10b. Six routes go through the tunnel and 9 routes go over the bridge; a total of 15 routes from the professor's home to the university.

Extensions

9. The diagram below represents a grid of city streets. Officer Hansel is at point A when he gets a call about a crime in progress at point B.

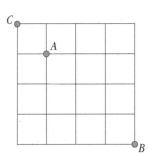

a. List five different shortest routes that Officer Hansel could take to the crime scene. Describe each route with a string of letters specifying one-block moves. For example, Officer Hansel could go east, then south, then south, then east, then south, and then east. You would indicate this by writing ESSESE.

b. How many different shortest routes are there? Explain.

c. Officer Valdez is at point C. How many different shortest routes could she take to the crime scene?

10. The diagram on the next page shows the routes a professor who lives in Detroit, Michigan, could take to the University of Windsor in Ontario, Canada.

a. Draw a simple network with nodes and edges to model this situation.

b. Use your network to find the number of possible routes from the professor's home to the university.

10a.

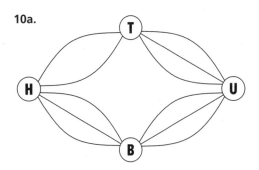

c. How many different routes could the professor take from the university to her home?

d. How many different round-trip routes could the professor make between her home and the university?

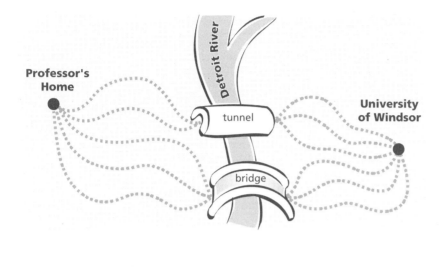

10c. Using similar reasoning, there are 15 routes from the university to the professor's home.

10d. There are 15 × 15 = 225 round-trip routes.

Investigation 3: Networks 35

Possible Answers

1. These problems have the same structure. You have to answer a question that starts, "How many ways . . . ?" To do so, you have to figure out how many occasions you are called upon to make a choice and how many choices there are for each occasion. Neighboring nodes on a network are like positions in a lock code, and the number of edge choices between consecutive nodes is equivalent to the number of choices for each position in a lock code. The problems are different in that the number of edges from a node is restricted only by the number of edges already assigned, while in a lock code the number of choices for each position either remains the same or is reduced by one each time because no repeats are allowed. Physically, the edges between each pair of nodes represent entirely different sets of choices while the numbers in a combination are selected from the same set of choices.

2, 3. See page 36i.

Mathematical Reflections

In this investigation, you explored the number of paths through given networks, and you designed networks that satisfied given conditions. These questions will help you summarize what you have learned:

1 How is finding the number of possible paths through a network similar to finding the number of possible lock combinations? How is it different?

2 **a.** Write a problem whose solution involves evaluating $5 \times 4 \times 3$.

b. Write a problem whose solution involves evaluating $20 \times 20 \times 20$.

3 Suppose you wanted to design a network with nodes A, B, and C; n edges; and the maximum number of paths from node A to node C through node B. How should you arrange the edges?

Think about your answers to these questions, discuss your ideas with other students and your teacher, and then write a summary of your findings in your journal.

In your mystery story, what situation might you include that would require the detective to find the number of paths through a network?

Tips for the Linguistically Diverse Classroom

Diagram Code The Diagram Code technique is described in detail in *Getting to Know Connected Mathematics*. Students use a minimal number of words and drawings, diagrams, or symbols to respond to questions that require writing. Example: Question 2a—A student might respond to this question by drawing a lock with three positions, a choice of five numbers, and the label *No repeats.*

TEACHING THE INVESTIGATION

3.1 • Making Rounds

Using the context of the guard's inspection rounds through the warehouse, this problem introduces students to networks. The term *network*, however, is not used until Problem 3.2.

Launch

Discuss the warehouse floor plan with the class, perhaps displaying Transparency 3.1A. Make sure students understand that any path from the first set of lockers to the second set must go through checkpoint B. Draw one path from A to B.

> If the guard follows this path from A to B, in how many ways can she complete her inspection round? *(5 ways)*
>
> Suppose the guard took a different path from A to B. In how many ways could she complete her inspection? *(5 ways)*
>
> Do the two paths represent different inspection rounds?

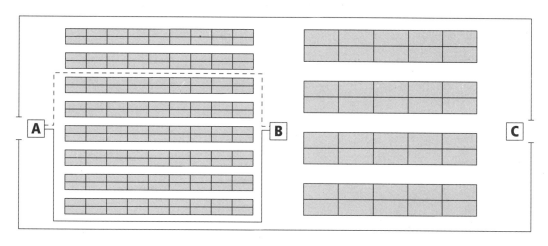

When students understand the floor plan in terms of the path choices that the guard can make as she patrols the warehouse, pose the question.

> If the guard makes only one inspection of the warehouse from checkpoint A to checkpoint C, what are the chances that she will pass Rodney's locker?

Have students work individually or in pairs on the problem and the follow-up.

Explore

Some students may make a sketch of the floor plan and try to draw or trace all the paths; their diagrams will soon become confusing. Others may begin to trace the paths in an organized way and realize that they can predict the number of paths without drawing them all.

If students are having trouble, suggest that they label each path from A to B and each path from B to C. They could use AB1, AB2, AB3, . . . , AB9 to label the paths from A to B and BC1, BC2, BC3, BC4, BC5 to label the paths from B to C, or a similar labeling scheme. From here, they can make an organized list or even a counting tree of all the possibilities.

As you circulate, ask students to explain the similarities between this network and the earlier counting problems. The clearer they can be in their explanations, the better they will understand the structure of these types of problems.

Summarize

Have students share their solutions and solution strategies. Most students should be feeling comfortable with solving such counting problems using multiplication.

When discussing the parallels between the network problem and the previous problems, it might be helpful to summarize the connections in a list. For example:

Lock-Combination Problem	Warehouse-Path Problem
How many numbers are in the code?	How many sections are in the warehouse?
How many choices are there for the first number in the code?	How many paths are there through the first section?
How many choices are there for the second number in the code?	How many paths are there through the second section?
Goal: To find the total number of codes consisting of one choice followed by another choice followed by. . . .	**Goal:** To find the total number of paths consisting of paths through the first section followed by paths through the second section.

3.2 • Networking

Students have seen how a graph and an equation can model a relationship. Now they will see how the warehouse floor plan can be stripped of unnecessary detail and reduced to a simple network model composed of nodes and edges. This problem introduces vocabulary about networks and reinforces some of what students have learned about modeling.

Launch

Discuss the network diagram shown in the student edition, or draw it on the board. Explain that the network represents the warehouse floor plan, and introduce the terms *node* and *edge*.

> What do the various parts of this diagram model? *(Edges represent aisles between lockers, and nodes represent checkpoints.)*

Notice that some of the edges are curved lines and some are straight lines. Does it matter whether an edge is straight or curved? *(No; each edge represents one way to travel from one node to the next.)*

Do you think the length of an edge is significant? *(No, the appearance of the edge doesn't matter; each edge represents one way to get from one node to another regardless of how the edges look.)*

Do you think a network can have an odd numbers of edges? *(yes)* An even number? *(yes)*

What do you think we need to know to find the total number of paths through a network? Do you think you can look at several networks and predict which has the greatest number of paths?

Let students share their ideas about these last two questions. Obviously, adding more edges will increase the number of paths, but placing the extra edges thoughtfully will have more impact. Students will be working with these concepts, so don't take the idea too far in this introduction.

Have students work in pairs on the problem and the follow-up.

Explore

Working in pairs will help students gain a better understanding of their work and the patterns they find. Encourage students to explain their findings to one another.

Summarize

Have students share what they have learned about networks.

How do we calculate the number of paths through a network?

By this time, students should see the multiplicative nature of these problems and understand that they have the same mathematical structure as all the previous counting problems.

Can you predict by looking at a network whether it will have an odd or an even number of paths? *(Yes; we can tell from the numbers to be multiplied whether the answer will be odd or even. If the numbers are all odd, the number of paths will be odd.)*

Discuss the follow-up questions, making sure students understand that in a round trip from A to C and back to A, four choices are made. Keep the initial discussion concrete by having students give specific round-trip paths. Then generalize the idea by multiplying the choices for each edge as before: for part A, $1 \times 8 \times 8 \times 1 = 64$ round trips.

3.3 • Designing Networks

Students have found the number of paths through several networks. In this problem, the task is the reverse: given a specific number of nodes and edges, students are challenged to create a network fitting the constraints. They will also inspect a network in which values are assigned to the edges.

Launch

To introduce the class to this new type of problem, read through part A as a class.

> How many nodes are your networks supposed to have? *(3)* How many edges? *(12)*

Students are to draw at least three networks that fit these constraints, look for patterns in their results, and use their observations to find the network with 3 nodes and 12 edges that has the maximum number of paths. In part B, they repeat the task for networks with 4 nodes and 12 edges.

Ask students to begin work on part A individually.

Explore

Have students work on part A and then share their ideas with their partners to find the maximum number of paths. (The maximum number of paths is called the *maximal network*; you may or may not want to use this term with students.) Have them repeat the process for part B. Students can do the follow-up questions as soon as they finish the problem.

Help students who are having trouble to draw one network that fits the conditions. Ask them to draw three more, finding the number of paths through each and looking for patterns.

Summarize

As students describe their networks for part A, draw them on the board or the overhead until all 11 are displayed. Make an organized list of the number of paths from A to C through B. Include the multiplication calculations to demonstrate the pattern.

Edges from A to B	Edges from B to C	Paths from A to C
1	11	$1 \times 11 = 11$
2	10	$2 \times 10 = 20$
3	9	$3 \times 9 = 27$
4	8	$4 \times 8 = 32$
5	7	$5 \times 7 = 35$
6	6	$6 \times 6 = 36$
7	5	$7 \times 5 = 35$
8	4	$8 \times 4 = 32$
9	3	$9 \times 3 = 27$
10	2	$10 \times 2 = 20$
11	1	$11 \times 1 = 11$

Describe any patterns in the table that would help you to write an equation for the number of paths through the network.

Help students to see these patterns:

- As the number of edges from A to B increases at a constant rate, the number of edges from B to C decreases at a constant rate.

- The number of edges from B to C is 12 minus the number of edges from A to B.

- The sum of the edges from A to B and the edges from B to C is 12.

- The total number of paths increases and then decreases "symmetrically."

From this information, lead the class in writing an equation for the total number of paths.

Suppose we let n stand for the number of edges from A to B in this network. What expression would represent the number of edges from B to C? *(12 – n)*

Let P stand for the number of paths through this network. Can you use what you have learned to write an equation for finding the number of paths?

The total number of paths can be found by multiplying the number of edges from A to B by the number of edges from B to C, which is represented by the equation $P = n(12 - n)$.

Does this equation look familiar? What would the graph of this equation look like?

The equation is quadratic, and the graph is a parabola that opens downward. You might graph the equation on the overhead graphing calculator or ask students to graph it on their own calculators. The points plotted below are the discrete values that make sense in the problem; the curve models the relationship.

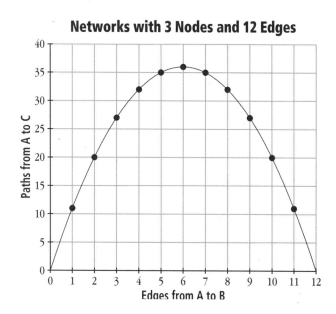

Networks with 3 Nodes and 12 Edges

What does the maximum point on the parabola represent? *(The maximum point represents the maximum value for the number of paths. When the number of edges from A to B is 6, the number of paths from A to C is $6 \times 6 = 36$.)*

For the Teacher: Maximum Area vs. Maximum Number of Paths

This problem has the same mathematical structure as the maximum-area problems that students studied in the unit *Frogs, Fleas, and Painted Cubes.* In each situation, the object is to find two numbers whose sum is fixed and whose product is as great as possible. The equation $A = l(12 - l)$ represents the area of a rectangle with a side of length l and a perimeter of 24. The rectangle with the greatest area is represented by the maximum point on the related parabola.

You may want to challenge students to look back at the maximum-area problems and study how they are related to this network problem.

As a class, perform a similar analysis for part B. You will not want to draw all 55 possible networks, but you might begin an organized list of the number of paths from A to C through B.

Edges from A to B	Edges from B to C	Edges from C to D	Paths from A to D
1	1	10	$1 \times 1 \times 10 = 10$
1	2	9	$1 \times 2 \times 9 = 18$
1	3	8	$1 \times 3 \times 8 = 24$
⋮			
2	1	9	$2 \times 1 \times 9 = 18$
2	2	8	$2 \times 2 \times 8 = 32$
2	3	7	$2 \times 3 \times 7 = 42$
⋮			
3	1	8	$3 \times 1 \times 8 = 24$
3	2	7	$3 \times 2 \times 7 = 42$
3	3	6	$3 \times 3 \times 6 = 54$
⋮			

If you want to design a network with a given number of nodes and edges and the maximum number of paths, what should you try to do? *(Make the number of paths between each pair of consecutive nodes the same; if the edges can't be distributed evenly, balance them as much as possible.)*

Have students share their answers to the follow-up questions.

Additional Answers

Answers to Problem 3.1 Follow-Up

1. There would be $15 \times 12 = 180$ paths from A to C through B. If Rodney's locker is small, 12 paths would pass by it and the probability that the guard would not pass it would be $\frac{168}{180} \approx 0.93 \approx 93\%$. If Rodney's locker is large, 15 paths would pass by it and the probability that the guard would not pass it would be $\frac{165}{180} \approx 0.92 \approx 92\%$.

2. Answers will vary. Most students will comment on the fact that choices were counted and multiplied in all the problems. Some may mention that face descriptions, license plates, and lock codes can be listed while warehouse paths must be drawn (though the paths can be labeled and then listed).

Answers to Problem 3.3

A. 1. Possible answer:

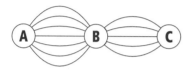 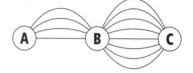 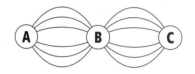

2. The number of paths from A to C is the product of the number of edges from A to B and the number of edges from B to C.

Edges from A to B	Edges from B to C	Paths from A to C
7	5	35
4	8	32
6	6	36

3. The network with the maximum number of paths is the third one drawn in part a. Of all the pairs of whole numbers that add to 12, the product of 6 and 6 is the greatest.

B. The network with the maximum number of paths has four edges between each pair of consecutive nodes. Of all the groups of three numbers that add to 12, the product $4 \times 4 \times 4$ is the greatest, for a total of 64 paths.

ACE Answers

Applications

3. Possible networks:

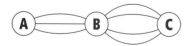 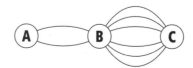 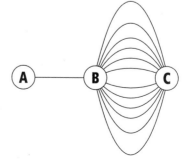

4. Possible networks:

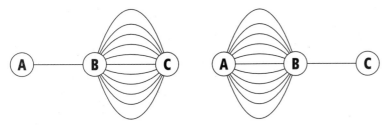

6. Possible answers:

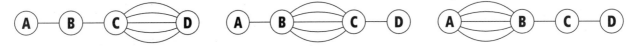

Extensions

9b. There are 20 shortest routes. Students might make an organized list of possibilities, for example:

EEESSS	SEEESS
EESESS	SEESES
EESSES	SEESSE
EESSSE	SESEES
ESEESS	SESESE
ESESES	SESSEE
ESESSE	SSEEES
ESSEES	SSEESE
ESSESE	SSESEE
ESSSEE	SSSEEE

Students might make a counting tree; at each branch, decisions are based on what can be done on the grid:

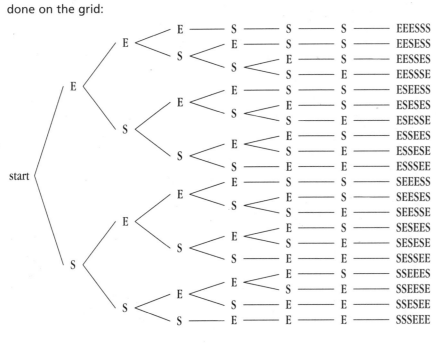

Mathematical Reflections

2a. Because the numbers decrease by 1 each time, this could be a lock combination with three positions, a choice of five numbers, and no repeats. (Note: Students might construct problems that are quite different in context but have the same structure.)

2b. This could be a network problem with four nodes and 20 edges between each pair of consecutive nodes. It could also represent a three-digit combination for a lock with 20 marks on its dial and repeats allowed.

3. If the number of edges, n, is even, divide the number by 2 to find the number of edges to use between nodes A and B and between nodes B and C. If n is odd, find the two numbers that differ by 1 and add to n and use these two numbers as the numbers of edges. (Note: Using algebraic notation, we can divide $n - 1$ by 2 and add 1. The two numbers of edges will be $\frac{n-1}{2}$ and $\frac{n-1}{2} + 1$. They will be consecutive integers that sum to n.)

Deciding Whether Order Is Important

This investigation teaches students to exercise care when using multiplication as a way of counting. Through their work, students learn that the context of a problem is crucial, as it determines whether possibilities such as 1-2 and 2-1 are to be counted as the same outcome or different outcomes. The two problems do not formalize counting procedures in which order does not matter, but they will help students realize the importance of considering, in each counting situation they encounter, whether order is important.

Problem 4.1, Playing Dominoes, poses the question of how many different double-six dominoes there are. Students often initially approach this problem using familiar but erroneous reasoning: there are seven possible dot, or pip, arrangements on each half of a domino, consisting of 0, 1, 2, 3, 4, 5, or 6 pips, so there ought to be $7 \times 7 = 49$ different dominoes. This reasoning overlooks the fact that domino halves are not ordered as first and second (lock codes, telephone numbers, most lottery tickets, and the like are). The first corrective reaction is often to simply divide 49 by 2, but that results in a fraction. Thus students are drawn to analyze the situation more carefully. By sketching or examining a full set of dominoes, they can see how their reasoning went astray. The image of an organized set of dominoes offers opportunities for students to make connections with algebraic and geometric concepts that will help them to think about the situation and solve the problem.

In Problem 4.2, Choosing Locks, students analyze another situation in which order is not important: selecting a set of objects from a larger collection.

Mathematical and Problem-Solving Goals

- **To identify the difference in the structure of problems in which order is not important from those in which it is**

- **To create a model to clarify a situation**

- **To generalize a pattern**

Materials		
Problem	**For students**	**For the teacher**
All	Graphing calculators	Transparencies: 4.1A to 4.2 (optional)
4.1		Set of dominoes or set of overhead dominoes (provided as a blackline master)

Deciding Whether Order Is Important

Detective Curious considered the possibility that the locker robbery may have taken place while the security guard and her friend were playing dominoes. She reasoned that they may have been so involved in their game that they would not have noticed a disturbance among the lockers.

4.1 Playing Dominoes

A domino is a rectangular tile divided into halves. On a standard *double-six* domino, each half contains from 0 to 6 dots, called *pips*. A complete set of dominoes contains one domino for each possible combination of halves.

What are possible halves?   0 to 6 (7 options)

Estimate!

4.1

Playing Dominoes

At a Glance

Grouping:
small groups

Launch

- Display a few double-six dominoes, and ask the class how many dominoes they think are in a set.
- Have groups of two to four work on the problem and follow-up.

Explore

- Ask students who calculate 7×7 to make a list or draw a picture of all the possibilities.

Summarize

- Have students share their solution strategies, and make sure everyone sees why 7×7 gives an incorrect answer.
- Discuss why the three problems are structurally different.
- Ask what strategies students discovered for making domino chains.

Assignment Choices

ACE questions 1, 2, 5, 9–13, and unassigned choices from earlier problems

Why not 7·7? (duplicates)

6⁻6 6⁻5 ··· 6⁻1 6⁻0 7

5⁻5 5⁻4 ·· 5⁻4 6

1⁻1 1⁻0 2 Q: When can
0⁻1 1³   you just
mult.

3, 8+4 = 28 a·6 works *only when order matters.*

‾‾ = 42 '
7·6   7 doubles

7·7 = 49
49−7 = 42 not counting
                duplicate

42/2 = 21   3⁻4 = 4⁻3

21
+ 7
‾‾‾
28

Problem 4.1

A. How many different dominoes are in a complete set?

B. The vending machines at Fail-Safe offer seven types of sandwiches and seven different drinks. The security guard wants to buy one sandwich and one drink. From how many combinations can she choose?

C. The security guard in a nearby storage warehouse can follow seven routes from checkpoint A to checkpoint B and seven routes from checkpoint B to checkpoint C. How many routes can he follow from checkpoint A to checkpoint C through checkpoint B?

D. Parts A–C each involve finding the number of ways to fill two positions when there are seven choices for each position. Compare the strategies you used to answer each part. How are the strategies similar? How are they different?

Problem 4.1 Follow-Up   *omit*

1. a. Is it possible to arrange *all* the different dominoes in a chain so that adjacent halves match and the domino half that starts the chain matches the domino half that ends the chain? If it is possible to make such a chain, give an example of a chain that works.

b. Is there more than one way to make such a domino chain? Explain.

2. How many pips are in a set of double-six dominoes?

Answers to Problem 4.1

A. There are 28 dominoes in a set. See the "Summarize" section for some possible solution strategies.

B. There are 7 × 7 = 49 combinations of a sandwich and a drink.

C. There are 7 × 7 = 49 routes from A to C through B.

D. You cannot simply multiply choices for positions in the domino problem because, although there are seven choices for each position, the order of each number pair can be reversed and should not be counted as a different domino. In the vending-machine problem, the position for sandwich can be filled only by a sandwich, not by a drink, whether the sandwich is chosen first or second. Likewise, the guard can follow a route from A to B only *before* following a route from B to C.

do Ice Cream Choices 1st 5 flavors - look for
patterns in triple scoop cone VS
bowl.

4.2 Choosing Locks

When you first tried to find the number of dominoes in a set, you may have counted some dominoes twice. If you used number pairs to represent the dominoes, you may have counted both 1–2 and 2–1. Because 1–2 and 2–1 represent the same domino, you need to count only one of the pairs. In counting situations like this, *order is not important*.

   1–2 and 2–1 represent the same domino.

When you consider possible zip codes, however, 94601 *is* different from 19460. In this situation, *order is important*.

  Al Gebra
12 Slope St
Oakland, CA 94601

  Cal Culus
8 Pi Blvd
Phoenixville, PA 19460

94601 and 19460 are zip codes for different cities

As you work on this problem and the follow-up questions, think carefully about whether the order of the choices is important.

Problem 4.2

After reviewing all he had learned about locks, the manager of Fail-Safe narrowed his choices to six models: the ACME CrimeStopper, the BurgleProof 2000, the Citadel, the Deterrent, the EverSafe, and the Fortress. He planned to bring samples of the locks to a meeting of Fail-Safe customers. Just before the meeting, he decided that offering so many choices would just confuse the customers. He chose two of the locks to bring to the meeting.

A. There are several ways the manager could have chosen the two locks. For example, he could have chosen the ACME CrimeStopper and the EverSafe. In how many different ways could the manager have chosen the two locks? Prove your answer is correct by listing all the possible pairs of locks.

B. If the manager had taken three locks to the meeting, in how many different ways could he have chosen them? Prove your answer is correct by listing all the possible sets of three locks.

C. How is finding the number of different ways the manager could have chosen the locks similar to and different from finding the number of lock combinations in Investigation 2?

Investigation 4: Deciding Whether Order Is Important **39**

4.2

Choosing Locks

◆ ◆ ◆ At a Glance

Grouping: *pairs, then groups of four*

Launch

■ Introduce the idea of whether order is important in a counting situation.

■ Have students think about the problem and then work in pairs.

Explore

■ Have pairs share ideas with another pair and then work as a group on the follow-up.

■ If students are struggling, help them to focus on the issue of order.

Summarize

■ Ask students to share their ideas about counting the locks.

■ Propose parallel situations in which order is and is not important to help students strengthen their understanding of the two situations.

Answers to Problem 4.1 Follow-Up

See page 46f.

Answers to Problem 4.2

The locks are referred to as A, B, C, D, E, and F for convenience.

A. The manager could have chosen 15 different pairs of locks: AB, AC, AD, AE, AF, BC, BD, BE, BF, CD, CE, CF, DE, DF, and EF.

B. The manager could have chosen 20 different sets of three locks: ABC, ABD, ABE, ABF, ACD, ACE, ACF, ADE, ADF, AEF, BCD, BCE, BCF, BDE, BDF, BEF, CDE, CDF, CEF, and DEF.

C. It is similar in that you are choosing elements to make up sets of three elements. It is very different in that the order in which you list the locks does not matter. The lock codes 123 and 321 are different; the sets of locks ABC and CBA are the same. This reduces the number of possibilities.

Assignment Choices

ACE questions 3, 4, 6–8, 14, and unassigned choices from earlier problems

Assessment

It is appropriate to use the quiz after this problem.

Investigation 4 **39**

■ **Problem 4.2 Follow-Up**

1. Six students are competing in the 100-meter dash. How many different arrangements of first-place, second-place, and third-place finishers are there?

2. How is question 1 similar to part B of Problem 4.2? How is it different?

Answers to Problem 4.2 Follow-Up

1. There are 6 × 5 × 4 = 120 different possible arrangements.

2. The problems are alike in that they are counting problems that involve "choosing" three elements from a set of six. They differ in that order matters in the race but does not matter in choosing a set of three locks.

Applications • Connections • Extensions

As you work on these ACE questions, use your calculator whenever you need it.

Applications

1. Suppose a special type of dominoes has from 0 to 8 pips on each half. How many different dominoes would be in a complete set?

2. Anya is forming a chain of double-six dominoes like the one described in Problem 4.1 Follow-Up. She started with the domino shown below. Now she must select a domino to connect to either side of this one. How many dominoes does she have to choose from? Remember, adjacent domino halves must match.

3. a. In how many different ways can two locks be chosen from a set of four locks?

    b. In how many different ways can two locks be chosen from a set of five locks?

    c. In how many different ways can two locks be chosen from a set of seven locks?

    d. Look at your answers to parts a–c and Problem 4.2. Describe a pattern you could use to predict the number of different ways two locks can be chosen from a set of *n* locks.

3d. The data are displayed in the table. To predict the number of ways two locks can be chosen from a given number of locks, add the integers from 1 up to one less than the number of locks in the set: $1 + 2 + 3 + \ldots + (n - 1)$.

Number of locks	Ways to choose two locks
4	6
5	10
6	15
7	21

(Note: As with the dominoes in Problem 4.1, the number of ways two locks can be chosen are the triangular numbers. They can be described by the rule $\frac{n^2 - n}{2}$ or $\frac{1}{2}n^2 - \frac{1}{2}n$, where *n* represents the number of locks.)

Answers

Applications

1. Students' solution methods will vary. As there are 9 dominoes with at least one blank half, 8 other dominoes with at least one half with one pip, and so on, a set would contain 9 + 8 + 7 + 6 + 5 + 4 + 3 + 2 + 1 = 45 dominoes.

2. She could connect any of dominoes 1-0, 1-1, 1-2, 1-4, 1-5, 1-6 to the left side and any of 3-2, 3-3, 3-4, 3-5, 3-6, 3-0 to the right side. So, she has 6 to choose from for each side, or 12 in all.

3. The locks are designated with letters—A, B, C, and so on—to simplify listing.

3a. Noting that order does not matter, 6 pairs can be drawn: AB, AC, AD, BC, BD, and CD. Or, 3 + 2 + 1 = 6 pairs.

3b. 10 pairs can be drawn: AB, AC, AD, AE, BC, BD, BE, CD, CE, and DE. Or, 4 + 3 + 2 + 1 = 10 pairs.

3c. 21 pairs can be drawn: AB, AC, AD, AE, AF, AG, BC, BD, BE, BF, BG, CD, CE, CF, CG, DE, DF, DG, EF, EG, and FG. Or, 6 + 5 + 4 + 3 + 2 + 1 = 21 pairs.

Connections

4a. Designating the friends by the letters A, B, C, D, and E, there are ten ways for Kyle to choose three friends (note that order does not matter): ABC, ABD, ABE, ACD, ACE, ADE, BCD, BCE, BDE, and CDE.

4b. There is a 1 in 10, or 10%, probability that he will choose any particular set of three friends.

5. See below right.

6a. Each person on one team shook hands with four people, making 16 handshakes in all. None of these are doubles because the team members are shaking hands with the *other* team.

Connections

4. Kyle just bought a new car. His friends Alexis, Bob, Carlos, Emile, and Frankie all want to ride with him to the football game, but he can take only three people with him.

  a. Kyle decides to choose three friends by randomly drawing names. He writes the five names on slips of paper and puts them in his cap. In how many ways can he choose three of the five friends?

  b. What is the probability that he will choose Alexis, Carlos, and Emile?

5. a. Al, Betty, and Conrado meet and shake hands. If each person shakes hands with everyone else, how many handshakes take place? Explain.

  b. Al, Betty, Conrado, and Ezra meet and shake hands. If each person shakes hands with everyone else, how many handshakes take place? Explain.

  c. Twenty people meet and shake hands. If each person shakes hands with everyone else, how many handshakes take place? Explain.

  d. How is finding the number of handshakes exchanged among a group of people similar to finding the number of different dominoes in a set? How is it different?

  e. How is finding the number of handshakes exchanged among a group of people similar to finding the number of two-number lock combinations? How is it different?

6. a. Before the championship match, the four members of the East High quiz-bowl team exchanged handshakes with the four members of the West High team. Each member of one team shook hands with each member of the other team. How many handshakes took place?

5a. Three handshakes take place: Al shakes with Betty and Conrado, and Betty and Conrado shake. (Note: Reasoning that each person shakes hands with two others, making 3 × 2 = 6 shakes, double-counts each handshake.)

5b. Six handshakes take place: Al shakes with Betty, Conrado, and Erza; Betty shakes with Conrado and Erza; and Conrado and Erza shake. Or, there are 3 + 2 + 1 = 6 handshakes.

5c. 190 handshakes take place. 20 × 19 = 380 counts every shake twice, and 380 ÷ 2 = 190.

5d. The handshake problem is similar to the domino problem—matching each person with every other person only once—except that it does not allow "doubles" in which people shake hands with themselves.

5e. The handshake problem is similar to finding two-number lock combinations in that two people shaking hands is like a two-number combination. It is different in that when two people shake hands, only one handshake occurs; whereas the two numbers in a combination can be pressed in two orders, making two different combinations.

b. The seven members of the North High debate team shook hands with the seven members of the South High team. Each member of one team shook hands with each member of the other team. How many handshakes took place?

c. The nine members of the Miller Middle School swim team exchanged high fives with one another after Tuesday's meet. How many high fives took place?

d. Which of the problems in parts a–c is most similar to finding the number of different dominoes in a set? Explain your answer.

e. Which of the problems in parts a–c is most similar to finding the number of two-number combinations for a push-button lock with repeats allowed? Explain your answer.

7. Donae made a chart to help her find the number of different dominoes in a set.

	0	1	2	3	4	5	6
0	(0, 0)	(0, 1)	(0, 2)	(0, 3)	(0, 4)	(0, 5)	(0, 6)
1	(1, 0)	(1, 1)	(1, 2)	(1, 3)	(1, 4)	(1, 5)	(1, 6)
2	(2, 0)	(2, 1)	(2, 2)	(2, 3)	(2, 4)	(2, 5)	(2, 6)
3	(3, 0)	(3, 1)	(3, 2)	(3, 3)	(3, 4)	(3, 5)	(3, 6)
4	(4, 0)	(4, 1)	(4, 2)	(4, 3)	(4, 4)	(4, 5)	(4, 6)
5	(5, 0)	(5, 1)	(5, 2)	(5, 3)	(5, 4)	(5, 5)	(5, 6)
6	(6, 0)	(6, 1)	(6, 2)	(6, 3)	(6, 4)	(6, 5)	(6, 6)

a. What do the number pairs on the diagonal represent?

b. Do (2, 3) and (3, 2) represent the same domino or different dominoes?

c. How are the dominoes represented by pairs *above* the diagonal related to the dominoes represented by pairs *below* the diagonal?

d. Explain how you could use the chart to find the number of different dominoes in a set.

e. Write a general equation for the number of different dominoes, d, in a set if each domino has from 0 to n pips on each half.

7d. Possible answer: There are $7 \times 7 = 49$ dominoes represented. Subtracting the 7 doubles in the diagonal leaves 42. In these 42, each nondouble is represented twice, meaning there are 21 nondoubles. Adding the 7 doubles makes $21 + 7 = 28$ dominoes.

7e. Possible answer: There are $n + 1$ possibilities for each half, 0, 1, 2, 3, . . . , n. Each row of a chart would have n nondouble entries. The chart would have $n + 1$ rows, for a total number of nondouble entries of $n(n + 1)$. Each of these is listed twice, so this represents $\frac{n(n + 1)}{2}$ different dominoes. There are $n + 1$ doubles, so the total number of dominoes is $d = \frac{n(n + 1)}{2} + (n + 1)$. [Note: This can be reasoned about in other ways to produce different but equivalent expressions, including $\frac{(n + 1)(n + 2)}{2}$.]

6b. A total of $7 \times 7 = 49$ handshakes took place.

6c. Each person is involved in 8 high fives, but this counts each high five twice, so $\frac{9 \times 8}{2} = 36$ high fives were exchanged. Or, the first person is involved in 8, the next is involved in 7, the next is involved in 6, and so on for $8 + 7 + 6 + 5 + 4 + 3 + 2 + 1 = 36$ high fives.

6d. The high-fives problem is most similar to the dominoes problem because, for example, person 1 high-fiving with person 2 is the same as person 2 high-fiving with person 1, which is equivalent to domino 1-2 being the same as domino 2-1.

6e. The handshake problems are most similar to the push-button lock problem because, for example, person 1 on one team shaking hands with person 1 on the other team is equivalent to pressing the same button twice.

7a. The number pairs on the diagonal represent the doubles.

7b. They represent the same domino.

7c. Each domino represented above the diagonal is also represented below it—for example, (0, 5) and (5, 0) represent the same domino.

8a. The number pairs on the diagonal represent people shaking hands with themselves, handshakes that should not be counted.

8b. These represent persons 2 and 3 shaking hands with each other and should be counted only once.

8c. The entries above (or the entries below) the diagonal represent 21 different handshakes.

8d. Each person must shake hands with $n - 1$ people, a total of $n(n - 1)$ handshakes. However, this counts each handshake twice, so the actual number of handshakes for n people is $h = \frac{n(n - 1)}{2}$.

9a. Kari could have thought of the number of pips on the right half of a domino as column entries and the number on the left half as row entries. The dark squares represent doubles.

9b. For n pips, there are $n + 1$ rows and $n + 1$ columns. The equation counts every space in the array, $(n + 1)^2$; subtracts the spaces on the diagonal, $n + 1$; takes half the result; and adds the spaces on the diagonal back in. This is equivalent to counting half of the nondouble entries in the chart shown in question 7 and adding in those on the diagonal.

8. The chart in question 7 can also represent the number of handshakes exchanged among a group of seven people. Use this interpretation of the chart to answer parts a–d.

   a. What do the number pairs on the diagonal represent?

   b. What do the pairs (2, 3) and (3, 2) represent?

   c. How many different handshakes are represented in the chart? Explain.

   d. Write a general equation for the number of handshakes, h, exchanged among n people.

9. Kari drew this diagram to help her visualize the problem of counting the dominoes in a set of double-six dominoes. The diagram leads to a general equation for the number of different dominoes, d, in a set if each domino has from 0 to n pips on each half.

Diagram   **General Equation**

$$d = \tfrac{1}{2}[(n + 1)^2 - (n + 1)] + n + 1$$

   a. How might Kari have been thinking about the problem?

   b. Explain how her diagram leads to the general equation.

   c. Describe the shape of the graph of the general equation.

9c. The graph is an increasing curve. If negative values of n are graphed, it will be clear that the graph is a symmetric parabola that decreases and then increases.

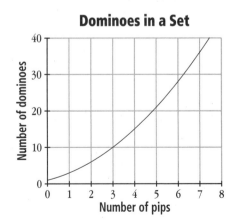

Dominoes in a Set

Extensions

In 10–14, use the following information: The tiles in the Tri-Ominoes® game are shaped like triangles. Each corner of a tile contains the number 0, 1, 2, 3, 4, or 5. A Tri-Ominoes game contains a tile for every combination of three numbers.

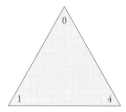 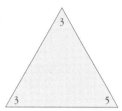

10. How many tiles contain exactly two 1s? Explain how you found your answer.

11. How many tiles contain exactly one 1? Explain how you found your answer.

12. How many tiles contain at least one 1? Explain how you found your answer.

13. How many tiles contain at least one 2? Explain how you found your answer.

14. Find the error in this argument: There are 21 Tri-Ominoes tiles that contain 1s. There must also be 21 tiles that contain 0s, 21 tiles that contain 2s, 21 tiles that contain 3s, and so on. So, the total number of tiles must be 6×21, or 126.

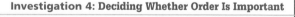

10. 5 tiles contain exactly two 1s: 110, 112, 113, 114, and 115 (011 and 101 represent the same tile as 110).

11. 15 tiles contain exactly one 1: 100, 102, 103, 104, 105, 122, 123, 124, 125, 133, 134, 135, 144, 145, and 155.

12. 21 tiles contain at least one 1: 15 contain exactly one 1, 5 contain exactly two 1s, and 1 contains three 1s.

13. 21 tiles contain at least one 2: 200, 201, 211, 202, 212, 222, 203, 213, 223, 233, 204, 214, 224, 234, 244, 205, 215, 225, 235, 245, and 255.

14. In this argument, some tiles are counted more than once. For example, 123 is counted in the list of tiles that contain 1s, the list of tiles that contain 2s, and the list of tiles that contain 3s. Multiplying 6×21 assumes that each group of 21 contains an entirely different set of tiles from the others, which is untrue.

1a. When counting the number of ways people might finish in a race, the order in which the people cross the finish line is important. When counting the number of possible license plates, the order of the characters on the plates is important.

1b. Jeff, Mali, and Glenda finishing a race in that order is different from Glenda, Jeff, and Mali finishing a race in that order. The license plate TXQ 75 is different from the license plate TQX 57.

2a. Choosing three students to represent the school at a meeting and choosing three colors to paint the blocks in a container are situations in which order is not important.

2b. Kai, Herschel, and Jason is the same group as Jason, Herschel, and Kai. When they attend the meeting, the group will contain the same three people no matter in what order their names are called. Choosing magenta, teal, and canary yellow is the same as choosing teal, canary yellow, and magenta.

Mathematical Reflections

In this investigation, you found the number of dominoes in a set and the number of ways a given number of locks can be chosen from a set of six locks. You discovered that in these counting situations, order is not important. These questions will help you summarize what you have learned:

1 **a.** In some counting situations, order is important. For example, when counting possible lock combinations, 2-3-4 is different from 3-4-2. Give two more examples of counting situations in which order is important.

b. Explain why order is important in your examples.

2 **a.** In some counting situations, order is not important. For example, when counting combinations of pizza toppings, a mushroom-and-onion pizza is the same as an onion-and-mushroom pizza. Give two more examples of counting situations in which order is not important.

b. Explain why order is not important in your examples.

Think about your answers to these questions, discuss your ideas with other students and your teacher, and then write a summary of your findings in your journal.

In your mystery story, what counting situations might your detective encounter in which order is not important?

Tips for the Linguistically Diverse Classroom

Diagram Code The Diagram Code technique is described in detail in *Getting to Know Connected Mathematics*. Students use a minimal number of words and drawings, diagrams, or symbols to respond to questions that require writing. Example: Question 1b—A student might respond to this question by drawing two sets of three stick figures approaching the finish line in a race and labeling the three figures in each set with the same three names but in different orders. Or, a student might draw two cars with the license plates TXQ 75 and TQX 75.

TEACHING THE INVESTIGATION

4.1 • Playing Dominoes

The structure of this problem is somewhat different from those of the other counting situations that students have explored. In a complete set of dominoes, which contains one domino for each possible combination of halves, there are seven choices for each position (domino half), two positions to fill, and repeats are allowed—however, combinations such as 0-1 and 1-0 represent the same domino. Students must think about counting in such a way that they do not count duplicates. Coming to terms with a pattern that will clarify this situation leads students to other counting models.

Launch

Have a set of dominoes on hand, or make a set for the overhead from Transparency 4.1A. Display a few dominoes to demonstrate the possibilities. For example, show the dominoes 0-1, 0-2, 0-3 and 4-0, 4-1, 4-2, 4-3. Students will get the idea, but they will not see enough of the set to simply count tiles.

> How many dominoes do you think there are in a complete set of double-six dominoes?

Take all guesses without comment. Then issue the challenge:

> With your group, predict how many dominoes are possible given that each half contains from 0 to 6 pips. Try to prove your answer in a way that will be convincing to someone who has not been studying this unit.

Have students work in groups of two to four on the problem and the follow-up.

Explore

Students' strategies for counting the number of dominoes may include making a list, drawing a diagram, or writing a formula. If they write a formula—most likely $7 \times 7 = 49$—ask them to confirm their answer by also making a list or a picture. This will lead them to another answer and force them to reflect on their original strategy. In trying to reconcile conflicting ideas, students may clarify for themselves how this problem is different from the lock-combination problems.

Listen to students' discussions, and choose students who have different strategies to explain their thinking in the summary.

The follow-up questions about chains of dominoes may prompt students to draw pictures of their solutions.

Summarize

Have students share their thinking. In particular, ask those whose first solution was incorrect to talk about where they think their error was. Make sure everyone understands what is wrong with the following reasoning:

> Why can't we calculate the number of dominoes in a set by noting that each half of a domino can contain one of seven numbers of pips—0, 1, 2, 3, 4, 5, or 6—and reason that because there are two halves, there must be 7 × 7 = 49 dominoes in a set? *(because this counts many of the dominoes twice)*

Here are four ways students may have approached the problem:

■ Some may have made an organized list, for example:

0-0	0-1	0-2	0-3	0-4	0-5	0-6
	1-1	1-2	1-3	1-4	1-5	1-6
		2-2	2-3	2-4	2-5	2-6
			3-3	3-4	3-5	3-6
				4-4	4-5	4-6
					5-5	5-6
						6-6

■ Some may have drawn a picture, for example:

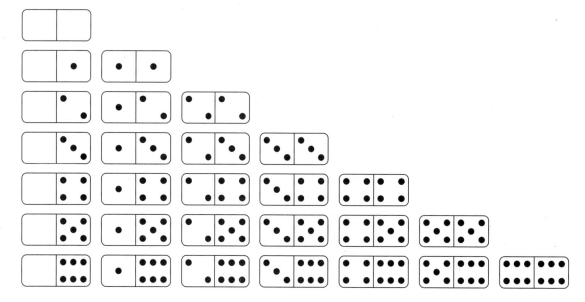

■ Some may start a list and then recognize that there will be 7 + 6 + 5 + 4 + 3 + 2 + 1 different dominoes in the list: 7 dominoes with at least one blank half, 6 other dominoes with at least one half with one pip, 5 other dominoes with at least one half with two pips, and so on. (This sequence leads to the triangular numbers, 1, 3, 6, 10, . . . , which students encountered in *Frogs, Fleas, and Painted Cubes*.)

■ Some may reason as follows: Multiplying 7 times 7 gives 49 dominoes, but this counts all nondouble dominoes twice. Subtracting the 7 doubles, we have counted 42 ÷ 2 = 21 dominoes twice. That means there are 49 − 21 = 28 dominoes in a set.

Parts B and C offer two more counting problems; part D asks students to compare the three problems. Students need time to articulate that although the structures of the problems are superficially the same, the domino problem has the added condition that order does not matter. Out of this discussion should arise a statement that the strategy of multiplying the numbers of choices is appropriate only in situations in which each position in a combination can be filled in a number of ways and order is important. This means that, in general, there is a position 1, a position 2, a position 3, and so on.

> What strategies did you use to make your domino chains?

Creating the chain is a fairly easy task once students realize that they must reserve a domino that will connect the end of the chain to the beginning and plan ahead for matching the numbers on that last domino. Some students may have observed that the doubles (0-0, 1-1, 2-2, and so on) can be disregarded until all the other dominoes are in a chain. Each double may then be placed between any two appropriate dominoes; for example, 3-3 might be placed between 2-3 and 3-4 or between 5-3 and 3-6.

4.2 • Choosing Locks

The dominoes problem raised the issue of counting situations in which applying the simple multiplication principle counts duplicates. The issue of whether order is important is the central difference between the counting situations in this investigation and all the counting problems students have previously explored. Students will now explore another problem in which order is not important.

Launch

Introduce the idea of whether order is important in a counting situation.

> When you count dominoes, is the order of the numbers on the halves important? (No; a 6-2 domino is the same as a 2-6 domino.)

> Is order important with numbers such as telephone area codes? (Yes, it is crucial: 602 and 206 are area codes for different locations.)

Explain that the manager has six types of locks to recommend. Point out that the locks begin with the letters A, B, C, D, E, and F, which will make working with them easier.

> As you work on this problem, remember to consider whether order is important.

Have students think about the situation individually before getting together in pairs.

Explore

Have students share their ideas with their partners. Then ask pairs to gather in groups of four to discuss ideas and answer the follow-up questions.

If any students are having difficulty with the problem, help them to focus on the issue of order by asking:

> Does the set of locks ABC and the set of locks CBA represent the *same* set?

For the Teacher: The Terminology of Combinatorics

The study of counting methods is called *combinatorics*. The issue of whether order is important is the central difference between *permutations* and *combinations*.

A *permutation* is an ordered arrangement of elements selected from a larger set of elements. If you select r elements from a set of n elements (with repeats not allowed), there are

$$n(n-1)(n-2) \cdots (n-r+1)$$

ways to make the selection if order matters.

A *combination* is a subset of a set of elements. The order in which the elements of the subset are listed does not matter. If you select a subset of r elements from a set of n elements (with repeats not allowed), there are

$$\frac{n(n-1)(n-2) \cdots (n-r+1)}{r(r-1)(r-2) \cdots (1)}$$

ways to choose an unordered set. The denominator of $r!$ divides out the repetitions of arrangements of r objects.

As these terms do not contribute to students' making sense of these issues, they are not presented in the student edition.

Summarize

Have several groups share their ideas about the problem. The main point that needs to emerge is that when students encounter a problem that requires clever counting, they must analyze the situation carefully to determine whether order is important.

With the help of the class, create a list of all the possibilities for parts A and B. This provides reinforcement for assuring that, for example, ABC and CBA are not both counted. The context makes it clear that a lock cannot be repeated, so designations such as AAB will not be on the list. You might add ABB to the list and ask whether it is appropriate to be sure students understand.

Ask questions to help students extend their understanding.

> Suppose the manager had *eight* models he was considering. How many different pairs of locks could he have chosen? *(There are now 28 different pairs.)*

> Compare this to a situation in which you are choosing codes from a set of eight letters with no repeats allowed. How many two-letter codes are possible? *(There are 8 × 7 = 56 different codes.)*

> How does the number of codes compare to the number of pairs of locks that could be chosen from a set of eight? Explain your answer.

Help students to see that the number of codes is twice the number of pairs of locks. This is because, for example, codes AB and BA are different, but AB and BA represent the same pair of locks. This means there will be half as many pairs of locks as codes when there are the same number of choices.

> Let's ask the same questions about sets of three locks and three-letter lock codes.

> Suppose the manager had eight models he was considering. How many different sets of *three* locks could he have chosen? *(This may be hard for students, but as the number of sets is 56, they can list them. It is worth the time to let students struggle with this question even if they need to finish it at home.)*

> How many three-letter codes could you choose from a set of eight letters with no repeats allowed? *(There are 8 × 7 × 6 = 336 different codes.)*

> How do the answers to these two problems compare? *(There are 336 ÷ 56 = 6 times as many codes as there are sets of locks.)*

Help students to understand why this makes sense.

> How many three-letter codes can be made from the letters C, D, and E? *(six: CDE, CED, DCE, DEC, ECD, and EDC)*

> How many sets of three locks contain locks C, D, and E? *(There is only one because CDE designates the same set of locks as the same three letters in any other order.)*

> How do these numbers compare? *(There are six three-letter codes to one set of locks, which explains why there are six times as many codes as there are sets of locks.)*

Carry this conversation as far as your class is interested.

For the Teacher: Translating These Ideas into Formulas

Some students may be intrigued by the idea of expressing these relationships symbolically.

For three-number sequences chosen from n numbers in which order *is* important and repeats are not allowed, we simply multiply to find the total: $n(n - 1)(n - 2)$. For three-number sequences chosen from n numbers in which order is *not* important and repeats are not allowed, we can divide the answer for the parallel situation in which order *does* matter by the number of times each set of numbers will be counted.

In the case of choosing sets of three numbers from a total of six numbers, there are $n(n - 1)(n - 2) = 6 \times 5 \times 4 = 120$ ways to choose when order is important, and $\frac{n(n - 1)(n - 2)}{6} = \frac{120}{6} = 20$ ways to choose when order is not important. The 6 in the denominator is derived from the number of ways three numbers can be arranged, or $3 \times 2 \times 1 = 6$.

Discuss the follow-up questions, which present another situation to help students focus on determining whether order is important.

Additional Answers

Answers to Problem 4.1 Follow-Up

1. a. yes; Possible chain: 0-0, 0-1, 1-1, 1-2, 2-2, 2-3, 3-3, 3-4, 4-4, 4-5, 5-5, 5-6, 6-6, 6-4, 4-2, 2-5, 5-3, 3-6, 6-2, 2-0, 0-3, 3-1, 1-4, 4-0, 0-5, 5-1, 1-6, 6-0

    b. There are many possible chains. Here is another: 0-0, 0-2, 2-2, 2-4, 4-6, 6-6, 6-5, 5-3, 3-1, 1-0, 0-3, 3-4, 4-4, 4-5, 5-5, 5-2, 2-6, 6-3, 3-3, 3-2, 2-1, 1-1, 1-5, 5-0, 0-6, 6-1, 1-4, 4-0

2. There are 168 pips in a set of dominoes. One way to think about this is to observe that each of the numbers 0 through 6 is represented eight times in a complete set. Therefore, the total is $8(0 + 1 + 2 + 3 + 4 + 5 + 6) = 168$. [Note: This turns out to be $\frac{n(n + 1)(n + 2)}{2}$, where n is the greatest number on a half of a domino. The expression $\frac{n(n + 1)}{2}$ sums the integers from 1 to n, and $n + 2$ tells how many of each number are in a set of dominoes.]

Wrapping Things Up

This investigation offers a review and a summary of the ideas students have encountered in *Clever Counting*. The unit began with an investigation of a burglary, an event that supplied a setting for students to develop their skills and reasoning ability about situations that call for counting. Students have worked on recognizing situations in which whole numbers can be multiplied or divided to answer counting questions. They have constructed organized lists to represent complex situations; recognized patterns that help to generalize situations; used diagrams, tables, and symbolic expressions to organize examples in listing and counting situations; made counting trees; analyzed situations to determine whether or not order is important; created networks to analyze certain kinds of counting situations; and used their growing knowledge to solve interesting problems. Now they will have a chance to examine all that they have learned about counting.

In Problem 5.1, Catching a Bicycle Thief, students return to the Fail-Safe warehouse to investigate another burglary. Drawing on what they have learned about counting in the previous investigations, students should now be able to ask and answer more sophisticated questions and have fun speculating what the second robbery reveals about the first.

Mathematical and Problem-Solving Goals

- **To recognize situations in which counting techniques apply**

- **To differentiate among situations in which order does and does not matter and in which repeats are and are not allowed**

- **To use a variety of models to clarify a solution**

- **To consider situations in which counting techniques would not apply**

- **To apply thinking and reasoning skills to an open-ended situation in which assumptions must be made and to create a persuasive argument to support a conjecture**

Materials		
Problem	For students	For the teacher
5.1	Graphing calculators	Transparency 5.1 (optional)
Unit Project	Labsheet UP (optional; 1 per student), Cuisenaire® rods (optional; as many as are available)	

INVESTIGATION 5

Wrapping Things Up

In the previous investigations, you learned techniques for solving counting problems. In this investigation, you will use what you have learned to help Detective Curious investigate a second robbery.

5.1 Catching a Bicycle Thief

Detective Curious was narrowing in on a suspect when another robbery took place at Fail-Safe. The detective was called to the scene on the morning the second burglary was discovered. During her investigation, she gathered the following information:

• Three mountain bikes were stolen from a locker rented by Bagged Bikes, Inc. The locker has a push-button lock with five buttons.

• The warehouse manager suspects that the night security guard committed the crime. The guard was on duty alone for several hours the night of the robbery. The guard claims she is innocent.

• There is an emergency exit at the end of the aisle in which Bagged Bikes' locker is located. The detective discovered tape over the latch of the exit, which prevented the door from closing properly.

• When the detective went to the manager's home to question him, she noticed a new mountain bike just inside his apartment door. The bike was the same model as one of the stolen bikes. The manager pointed out that mountain bikes are very popular and that many people own them.

At a Glance

Grouping:
small groups

Launch

■ Talk about the new robbery.

■ Discuss how groups will present their analyses.

■ Have groups of two or three work on the problem and follow-up.

Explore

■ As groups work, encourage them to use the mathematics they have learned about in their analyses.

Summarize

■ Have groups present their ideas, which should cover the issues of the push-button lock and the serial numbers.

Assignment Choices

ACE questions 1–17 and unassigned choices from earlier problems

• When the owner of Bagged Bikes checked the serial numbers for the stolen bikes, she found that the records had been smudged. She knew that each serial number consisted of three letters followed by six numbers, but she could read only the first two letters and the last four numbers of each.

Model	Serial number
Rocky Road	UM⋯ ⋯3245
Trail Blazer	UM⋯ ⋯4397
Rugged Rider	UM⋯ ⋯7711

Problem 5.1

You know as much as the detective does about counting combinations and calculating probabilities. Imagine that the detective asks you to help her with the case.

A. Which pieces of evidence would you investigate further? How would you proceed with your investigation?

B. What questions would you ask the security guard, the manager, or someone else involved in the case?

C. Does the evidence from the second robbery clear any of the suspects? Who are your suspects now? Why?

■ Problem 5.1 Follow-Up

1. a. One of the smudged serial numbers was UM _ _ _ 7711. The first blank represents a letter, and the other two blanks represent numbers. In how many ways can this serial number be completed?

b. The bike at the manager's home had the serial number UMZ567711. Based on your findings from part a, can you draw any conclusions about the manager's guilt or innocence? Explain.

Answers to Problem 5.1

A.   See page 56b.

B.   Answers will vary. Students might want to ask the security guard whether she has any witnesses for the time she was on duty and how many hours passed without any witnesses. They might want to ask the manager when he bought the mountain bike and whether he has evidence that he paid for it. They would also want to find out how the push-button lock works in order to be able to estimate how long it would take to open it.

C.   Answers will vary. Many students will have settled on the manager as being the prime suspect. They may hypothesize that the taped exit was the manager's attempt to throw suspicion on others. Some may decide that there is not enough evidence to prove an inside job.

2. a. Assume that all mountain bikes have serial numbers with three letters followed by six numbers. How many possible combinations are there for the first two letters and the last four numbers of the serial number for a mountain bike?

b. What are the chances that the serial number on the manager's bike would contain the sequence UM_ _ _7711?

c. Based on your findings, can you draw any conclusions about the manager's guilt or innocence? Explain.

Answers to Problem 5.1 Follow-Up

1. a. $26 \times 10 \times 10 = 2600$ ways

    b. There may be many bikes with serial numbers that match UM _ _ _ 7711, and they are all equally likely to be the stolen bike. If all 2600 of the possible serial numbers have been assigned, there is only a $\frac{1}{2600}$ probability that the manager has the stolen bike.

2. a. $26 \times 26 \times 10 \times 10 \times 10 \times 10 = 6,760,000$ possible combinations

    b. Assuming that each serial number is equally likely (and this might not be true for the location of the robbery), a random buyer would have a $\frac{2600}{6,760,000} = \frac{1}{2600}$ chance of getting a bike with a serial number containing the sequence UM _ _ _ 7711.

    c. The evidence seems to incriminate the manager, but students will have to deal with the fact that all the evidence is circumstantial. They may have creative ways to attempt to make the case stronger.

Answers

Applications

1a. With 3 types of containers (sugar cone, cup, and waffle cone) and 12 flavors, there are 3 × 12 = 36 different one-scoop orders.

1b. The $2 orders would consist of two scoops of ice cream in a waffle cone. The number of ways to get two scoops depends on whether the *order* of two different scoops is considered. If students decide that order does not matter, there are 78 different possibilities ($\frac{12 \times 12 - 12}{2} + 12$). If they decide that order does matter (that is, that an eggnog/kiwi cone is different from a kiwi/eggnog cone), there are 12 × 12 = 144 possibilities, minus the 12 orders that consist of two scoops of a single flavor, for 132 possibilities.

1c. The $1.75 orders are similar to the $2.00 orders except that there are two choices for container (sugar cone or cup), making twice as many possibilities: 156 if order does not matter and 264 if it does.

2. 10 × 10 × 10 = 1000 passwords

3. 26 × 10 × 10 × 10 = 26,000 passwords

As you work on these ACE questions, use your calculator whenever you need it.

Applications

1. Detective Curious took her team of detectives out for ice cream. The ice cream shop offers 12 flavors of ice cream.

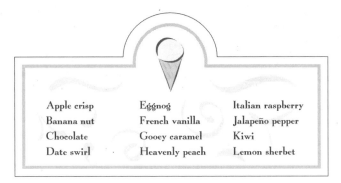

Apple crisp	Eggnog	Italian raspberry
Banana nut	French vanilla	Jalapeño pepper
Chocolate	Gooey caramel	Kiwi
Date swirl	Heavenly peach	Lemon sherbet

A single scoop of ice cream costs $1.25, and two scoops cost $1.75. A cup or a sugar cone is included in the price of the ice cream; a waffle cone is 25¢ extra.

a. How many different one-scoop orders are possible?

b. How many different $2 orders are possible?

c. How many different $1.75 orders are possible?

In 2–6, use this information: To keep data on computer networks secure, many computer systems require users to enter a password.

2. If a computer system accepts only three-digit passwords, such as 314 or 007, how many passwords are possible?

3. If a computer system accepts only passwords consisting of one letter followed by three numbers, such as Z300 and E271, how many passwords are possible?

4. If a computer system accepts only two-letter passwords, such as AZ and CC, how many passwords are possible?

5. If a computer system accepts only passwords consisting of two letters followed by three numbers, such as AB123 and LP333, how many passwords are possible?

6. The computer system at Jamie's school accepts only six-character passwords. A password may be all letters, all numbers, or a combination of numbers and letters. For example, A23BC7 and JTFEY1 are possible passwords. Jamie forgot his password and is attempting to log onto the system by guessing six-character sequences. How many such combinations are possible?

Connections

7. Akili, Beatrice, Consuelo, and David eat lunch together every day.

   a. Use the letters A, B, C, and D to represent the students. List all the possible orders in which the four students could stand in the lunch line.

   b. Make a counting tree for finding all the possible orders in which the four students could stand in the lunch line. How many paths are there through the branches of your tree?

   c. If Elena joined the students for lunch, in how many possible orders could the five students stand in line?

---

4. $26^2 = 676$ passwords

5. $26^2 \times 1000 = 676,000$ passwords

6. $36^6 = 2,176,782,336$ combinations

Connections

7a. ABCD, ABDC, ACBD, ACDB, ADBC, ADCB, BACD, BADC, BCAD, BCDA, BDAC, BDCA, CABD, CADB, CBAD, CBDA, CDAB, CDBA, DABC, DACB, DBAC, DBCA, DCAB, DCBA

7b. There are 24 paths through the tree. See below left.

7c. There are 5 ways for the first position in line to be filled, 4 for the second, 3 for the third, 2 for the second, and 1 for the last, for $5 \times 4 \times 3 \times 2 \times 1 = 120$ orders.

7b.

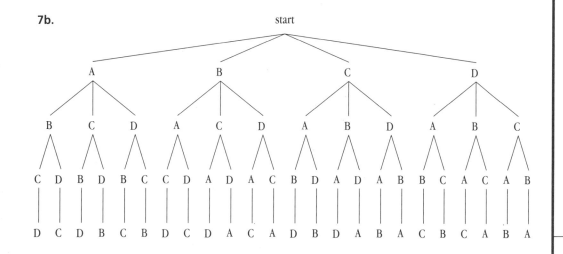

8a. $5 \times 4 \times 3 \times 2 \times 1 = 120$ ways

8b. Answers will vary. Students might refer to a counting tree.

8c. This chart works for only two characteristics, or two dimensions: one represented by rows and one represented by columns. It would not be useful for counting facial characteristics because there are more than two characteristics with attributes.

8d. For the same reason, this two-dimensional chart would not be useful for counting three-number lock combinations.

8. When counting two-choice combinations, it often helps to make a chart like the one below. Detective Curious made this chart to help her assign tasks to her detectives. The names of the detectives are listed across the top of the chart, and the tasks are listed along the side. Each box in the chart represents a possible assignment. The mark indicates that Clouseau has been assigned the task of gathering descriptions.

	Clouseau	Hercule	Jane	Sherlock	Jessica
determining lock combinations					
investigating license plates					
conducting interviews					
gathering descriptions	✓				
researching phone numbers					

a. In how many ways can Detective Curious make the assignments if each detective is to have a different task?

b. What other method could you use to count the possible ways to assign the tasks?

c. Would this type of chart be useful for counting the number of different faces a police artist could draw by combining eye, nose, hair, and mouth attributes? Explain.

d. Would this type of chart be useful for counting the number of possible three-number lock combinations? Explain.

9. Mr. Saari makes a chart each semester for recording grades. He writes student names down the left column of the chart, and lists assignments, tests, quizzes, and projects along the top.

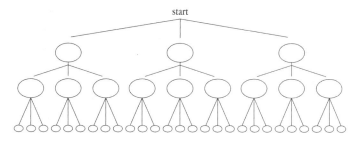

	Q1	Q2	Test 1	Proj 1
L. Alavosus	18	24	85	93
D. Alvarez	23	21	81	100
N. Chan	21	15	92	89

a. Next semester, Mr. Saari plans to give 5 quizzes, 3 tests, 10 homework assignments, and 3 projects. How many columns will he need to record all the scores?

b. If Mr. Saari has 28 students, how many score boxes will be filled at the end of the semester? Assume he will record a 0 for any missed or incomplete assignment, quiz, test, or project.

c. **i.** If Mr. Saari has 35 students, how many score boxes will be filled at the end of the semester?

ii. Would adding one student or adding one test cause the greater increase in the number of score boxes filled?

10. Write a problem that could be answered by using this counting tree. Copy the counting tree, and label it to represent the solution to your problem.

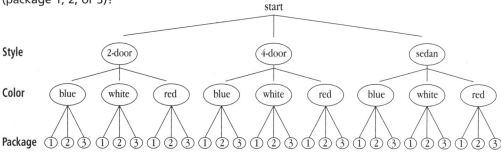

9a. He will need 5 + 3 + 10 + 3 = 21 columns.

9b. 28 × 21 = 588 boxes will be filled.

9c. **i.** 35 × 21 = 735 boxes will be filled.

ii. Adding one more test adds a column of 35 boxes while adding one more student adds a row of only 21 boxes.

10. See below left.

---

10. Possible answer: How many different combinations are there for a car that is offered in three styles with a choice of three colors and a choice of three accessory packages (package 1, 2, or 3)?

11. See below right.

Extensions

Note: Questions 12–16 have been simplified to make them easier for students to tackle. In reality, the numbers 411, 611, 911 are not allowed as prefixes or area codes, and 555 is not allowed as a prefix. Such restrictions change fairly frequently. You might suggest that students call the local telephone company to check current information.

12. There are 8 choices for the first number in the prefix and 10 choices for each of the other numbers. Thus, there are $8 \times 10^6 =$ 8,000,000 ways to complete the number, assuming all the numbers are allowed.

13. For each area code, there are 8,000,000 ways to complete the number, or 16,000,000 numbers in all.

14. There are $10^4 =$ 10,000 ways to complete the number, so there are 9999 phone numbers with the same area code and prefix as any given number.

15. There are $8^2 \times 10^8 =$ 6,400,000,000 possible phone numbers.

---

11. Write a problem that could be answered by using this counting tree. Copy the counting tree, and label it to represent the solution to your problem.

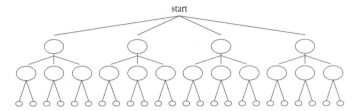

start

Extensions

In 12–16, use this information: In North America, a telephone number consists of a three-digit *area code*, followed by a three-digit *prefix*, followed by four more digits. For example, the telephone number of the White House in Washington, D.C., is (202) 456-1111.

(202) 456-1111

area code   prefix

The first digit of an area code and the first digit of a prefix must be greater than or equal to 2.

12. How many telephone numbers with an area code of 500 are possible?

13. Toll-free telephone numbers have an area code of 800 or 888. How many toll-free telephone numbers are possible?

14. How many telephone numbers with the same area code and prefix as your telephone number are possible?

15. How many different U.S. telephone numbers are possible?

---

11. Possible answer: Four people (Alan, Brenda, Carlos, and Deshon) will be randomly chosen for three committee positions: coordinator, recorder, and treasurer. The first row represents the four choices for coordinator, the second row represents the three remaining choices for recorder, and the third row represents the two remaining choices for treasurer.

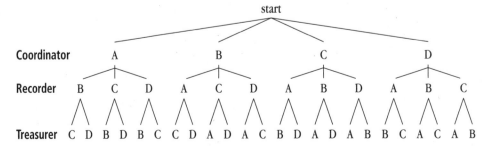

16. Telephone numbers mentioned in television shows and movies have the prefix 555. No actual phone numbers have this prefix. If you exclude phone numbers with the prefix 555, how many different U.S. phone numbers are possible?

Did you know?

As people within a particular area code add telephone lines for computer modems, fax machines, and cellular phones, more and more telephone numbers are needed. When all the possible numbers for an area code are taken, a new area code must be instituted. Until recently, all area codes started with digits from 2 to 9 and had 0 or 1 as the second digit. Now area codes can be any three-digit combination with a first digit greater than or equal to 2 except 411, 611, and 911.

17. A traveling salesman is trying to plan the least expensive route for visiting his customers. He needs to stop in ten cities on his trip. He can visit the cities in any order, but he doesn't want to visit the same city twice. He decides to list the cities in every possible order and then check the travel costs for each possibility.

    a. Do you think the salesman's plan of figuring out the cost for each possibility is a good one? Explain.

    b. Do you think a counting tree would help the salesman with his plan? Explain.

16. There are $(8 \times 10 \times 10) \times (1 \times 1 \times 1) \times (10 \times 10 \times 10 \times 10) = 8{,}000{,}000$ phone numbers with the prefix 555, leaving 6,392,000,000 possible phone numbers.

17a. There are 10 cities he can start with, 9 cities for the second choice, 8 for the third choice, and so on, for $10 \times 9 \times 8 \times 7 \times 6 \times 5 \times 4 \times 3 \times 2 \times 1 = 3{,}628{,}800$ possible orders. Obviously, listing all the possible orders is not a good way to proceed.

17b. A counting tree might help him begin to organize his thinking about the choices, but it would be too difficult to show all the possible orders.

Tips for the Linguistically Diverse Classroom

Rebus Scenario The Rebus Scenario technique is described in detail in *Getting to Know Connected Mathematics.* This technique involves sketching rebuses on the chalk-board that correspond to key words in the story or information that you present orally. Example: Some key phrases for which you may need to draw rebuses while discussing the "Did you know?" feature: *area code* [(619) 555-1234], *telephone lines* (lines coming from telephone poles), *computer modems, fax machines, and cellular phones* (sketches of them).

Possible Answers

1a. The choices are attributes for hair, eyes, nose, and mouth.

1b. The positions are the first number, the second number, and the third number.

1c. The choices are the first number, the second number, and the third number.

1d. The choices are a path from node A to node B, a path from node B to node C, and so on.

1e. The choices are a number of pips for one half of a domino and a number of pips for the other half of the domino.

2. If order is important, the number of ways a group of choices could be made or a set of positions could be filled is the product of the number of choices at each stage. For example, if there are a choices at the first stage and b choices at the second stage, there are $a \times b$ ways the choices could be made. If results with the same choices but in different orders are considered identical, we have to be careful to list them in a way that does not count duplicates. In the domino problem, for example, the product $a \times b$ results in duplicates.

3, 4. See page 56b.

In this unit, you learned techniques for counting the number of ways a group of choices can be made or a set of positions can be filled. These questions will help you summarize what you have learned:

1 Identify the choices or positions involved in each counting problem.

   a. finding the number of faces the police artist could draw (Problem 1.1)

   b. finding the number of license plates with three letters followed by three numbers (Problem 1.2)

   c. finding the number of three-number lock combinations (Problem 2.2)

   d. finding the number of paths through a network (Problem 3.2)

   e. finding the number of dominoes in a set (Problem 4.1)

2 State a rule or rules for finding the number of ways a group of choices could be made or a set of positions could be filled.

3 Explain how you can find the number of possibilities represented by a counting tree without counting the last set of branches.

4 A particular counting problem involves making three choices in order. There are a options for the first choice, b options for the second choice, and c options for the third choice. Explain how you would find the number of possible combinations of options.

Think about your answers to these questions, discuss your ideas with other students and your teacher, and then write a summary of your findings in your journal.

Describe how the detective in your story might use charts, graphs, or counting trees to explain his or her solution.

Tips for the Linguistically Diverse Classroom

Diagram Code The Diagram Code technique is described in detail in *Getting to Know Connected Mathematics*. Students use a minimal number of words and drawings, diagrams, or symbols to respond to questions that require writing. Example: Question 1b—A student might answer this question by drawing rows of boxes: drawing a different hairstyle in each of two squares for the first row, different eyes in each of four squares for the second row, different noses in each of four squares for the third row, and different mouths in each of three squares for the fourth row.

TEACHING THE INVESTIGATION

5.1 • Catching a Bicycle Thief

Students are faced with a new robbery and a new clue in this problem, and open-ended questions encourage them to decide what to investigate. For instance, they learn that the locker that was burglarized this time has a push-button lock; does that mean that the warehouse guard could have tried all the combinations? They are also given information about the serial numbers of bicycles and must think about whether they can apply that knowledge to identify a stolen bike with any degree of certainty.

Launch

Read through the new set of clues with the class. This problem does not introduce new concepts or unfamiliar contexts, so simply alert students to their roles. Explain that they are now assistant detectives and, working in their groups, they should decide what evidence they want to investigate, write questions to ask people involved in the case, and analyze their findings.

Decide with students how they will present their analyses of the evidence. Will they write and turn in reports, perhaps to be copied and shared? Will they prepare and make oral presentations with graphics to support their arguments?

The follow-up questions continue with the context of bicycle serial numbers. You may want to suggest that students write and answer additional follow-up questions about other topics that they believe need further investigation.

Have students work in groups of three or four on the problem and the follow-up.

Explore

Some groups will follow the structure of the problem and the follow-up and form their analyses quickly; others will probably take longer to analyze the evidence. Your role is to make sure they don't stray too far from the evidence and that their creativity is focused. Proposing a time limit may help them stay on task. Encourage them to use the mathematics they have learned rather than devising clever but unrelated solutions.

Summarize

Have groups present their ideas, which at a minimum should deal with the issues of the push-button lock and the serial numbers. Ask such questions as the following:

Does the push-button lock contribute to the insecurity of this locker? Why?

How did you count the lock codes?

Could the guard have cracked this combination more easily than that of the combination lock?

How did you count the possible serial numbers?

Does the number of possible serial numbers make the evidence against the manager weaker or stronger?

Additional Answers

Answers to Problem 5.1

A. Answers will vary. Students may see the need for determining how many combinations there are for the push-button lock and how long it would take to try them all. In Problem 2.1, they found that the number of possible lock sequences for this kind of lock is 320 and that it would take about 22 minutes (assuming 1 second per letter in the code) to try them all. If students assume, however, that one-letter codes and repeats *are* allowed, the number of possible lock sequences increases to 5 + 25 + 125 + 625 + 3125 = 3905 and the time it takes to try them all increases to 1(5) + 2(25) + 3(125) + 4(625) + 5(3125) = 18,555 seconds, or about 309 minutes, or about 5 hours. Students may mention checking the serial number on the bike found at the manager's home and finding the probability that it matches a serial number of one of the stolen bikes. They might also talk about checking out where Bagged Bikes' locker was located.

Mathematical Reflections

3. If you make a counting tree to represent choices for three different things, multiply the number of choices at each of the three stages to find the total number of possibilities. For example, a counting tree that represents the meals that can be selected from a menu offering three main courses, two side dishes, and three drinks would have $3 \times 2 \times 3 = 18$ final branches.

4. If order is important, multiply $a \times b \times c$ to find the number of possibilities. If order is not important, adjust this product for any duplicates of arrangements. For example, ABC may be a possibility; but ABC, ACB, BAC, BCA, CAB, and CBA are all the same if order is not important. The expression $a \times b \times c$ counts each of these six sequences. We need to eliminate the duplicates and leave a count of 1 for any arrangement of ABC. Since each three-letter sequence is represented on the list six times, we can divide by 6 so that each sequence is counted only once.

The Unit Project

Complete one of the projects described below.

Project 1: Writing a Detective Story

Throughout this unit, you have been recording ideas for a mystery story. Use your ideas to write a story about a detective's investigation of a crime. Your story should include some of the following:

- a cast of suspicious characters
- a detective with mathematical ability and an assistant who always needs explanations
- a lock combination
- a getaway vehicle
- different getaway routes
- a partially legible telephone number found at the scene of the crime

Your story must show the detective doing the following:

- counting combinations
- figuring out how long it would take to make, do, or check something
- using probability to show what is likely or unlikely to have happened
- using charts, graphs, or counting trees to explain his or her solution

Assigning the Unit Project

In this optional unit project, students apply what they have learned about counting. Students have a choice of two projects. Project 1 should appeal to students who enjoy creative writing. Project 2 involves manipulating objects to form patterns that lead to generalizations and should appeal to students who enjoy hands-on exploration. The project can be started while Investigation 5 is in progress.

In Project 1, Writing a Detective Story, students apply the ideas they have been developing for a mystery. Students will furnish the motive, the clues, and the characters. Their stories are to include examples of all the types of counting situations they have studied in the unit. This project can be used in place of the Unit Test as the final assessment of the unit.

In Project 2, Making Trains, students will apply to a counting situation what they know about finding patterns and writing equations. For this project, students will need a copy of Labsheet UP, Making Trains.

Talk to students about both projects and allow time for them to think about which they would like to pursue. Each project can be done by students individually. However, the final products will be better if you take class time, after students have their first drafts, to allow students working on the same project to gather in pairs and share ideas.

Ideas for assessing the projects can be found in the Assessment Resources section.

Project 2: Making Trains

In this project, you will make "trains" by joining "cars" of different lengths. A "car" is a rectangular strip of paper; a "train" is one car or two or more cars placed end-to-end. You will find the cars on Labsheet UP. Each car is labeled with a number that indicates its length in centimeters.

For each different car, find every possible train you can make with the same length as that car. Consider trains made from the same cars, but in a different order, to be different. This means that a 1-car followed by a 2-car is different from a 2-car followed by a 1-car. The drawing below shows the four trains that can be made with the same length as a 3-car.

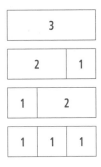

For each different car on the labsheet, record the length of the car and the number of trains with the same length as that car. Look for a pattern in your results. Write an equation for the relationship between the length of a car, L, and the number of trains with that length, N. Compare the pattern of change and the equation for this situation with the patterns and equations for other situations you have studied in this unit.

Write a paper two or three pages in length summarizing your findings.

Assessment Resources

Name _____   Date _____

1. Some license plates contain all numbers, some contain all letters, and some contain letters and numbers. Some combinations of letters are clever or amusing. Suppose a plate contains only three letters.

    a. How many possible three-letter sequences are there? Explain.

    b. How many of these three-letter sequences start and end with the same consonant and have a vowel (A, E, I, O, U) in the center? (A word that can be read forward and backward, such as POP, DAD, and GIG, is called a *palindrome*.) Explain your reasoning.

2. A certain lock has combinations consisting of three digits from 0 to 9. A number may not appear more than once in a combination.

    a. Make an *organized* list showing at least 12 combinations that start with 1.

    b. How many ways are there to choose the first number?

© Dale Seymour Publications®

   c.   How many ways are there to choose the second number?

   d.   How many ways are there to choose the third number?

   e.   How many possible combinations are there?

3.   A certain push-button lock consists of five numbers. To open the lock, five numbers must be pressed in the correct sequence. A number may not occur more than once in a sequence.

How many five-number sequences are possible? Explain how you found your answer.

Quiz

The network below contains nodes A, B, and C and five edges.

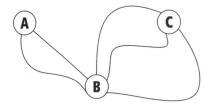

1. **a.** Design a network with nodes W, X, Y, and Z and exactly 11 edges. Each edge should connect nodes W and X, nodes X and Y, or nodes Y and Z.

    b. Record the total number of paths from node W to node Z in your network.

2. Design a network with nodes A, B, C, and D and exactly 11 edges that has the *maximum* number of paths from node A to node D.

3. Design a network with nodes J, K, L, and M and exactly 11 edges that has the *minimum* number of paths from node J to node M.

© Dale Seymour Publications®

Quiz

4. The buttons of a telephone contains letters as well as numbers.

   a. How many letters are on each button?

   b. Suppose your telephone number is 555-3276 and you would like to make it easy for people to remember. You want to be able to tell people that your number is 555-????, where the question marks represent letters that will give 3276 when dialed. How many combinations of letters are there for the sequence 3276?

   c. Write a word that will give 3276 when dialed.

5. Tad and his family are planning a vacation to explore their interest in the Civil War. Tad's research reveals 18 historic Civil War sites that he would like to see. He has the responsibility of determining the most efficient way to visit all 18 sites. His little brother suggests that he list all the possible orders and trace each of them on a map. Help Tad explain to his brother how many orders are possible and how much time this task would require if it takes 2 minutes to trace each order on a map.

© Dale Seymour Publications®

Assign these questions as additional homework, or use them as review, quiz, or test questions.

1. This diagram is a model of four emergency telephones positioned at strategic points along a patrol route in a high-security area. Nodes represent telephone locations, and edges represent possible segments of the guard's route. How many different routes can the guard take around the area?

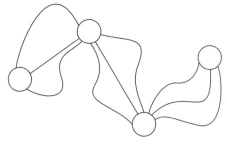

2. To play the Any-3 lottery game, players must choose three numbers from 1 to 30. The same number may not appear more than once in a selection. However, the order of the numbers is not important: 3-22-4 is the same as 4-3-22. Homer chooses the numbers 23, 15, and 2.

    a. How many ways are there to order 23, 15, and 2?

    b. What is the total number of possible selections in this lottery?

    c. What is the probability that Homer will win this lottery?

3. Suppose your school has the opportunity to send three students to Washington, D.C., to participate in a "Meet the President Day." The trip will cost $500 per student. There are 1127 students in your school. The principal wants to raise the money for the trip and wants each student to have a chance to represent the school, so she plans a lottery. Everyone who wants a chance to go on the trip pays $3 for a ticket, and no one can buy more than one ticket.

    a. The tickets contain a sequence of three numbers from 0 and 9, such as 0-9-2 and 3-2-2. How many different tickets are possible?

    b. Will enough money be collected if 500 students buy a ticket?

    c. To choose the winning combinations, the principal will draw three balls, one at a time, from a box containing balls numbered from 0 to 9. She will replace the ball after each draw. The student holding the ticket with a number sequence matching the numbers drawn will win. Three winners will be chosen. Are there any problems with the principal's plan?

© Dale Seymour Publications®

4. The prosecution in a trial has three witnesses who will give accounts that could make the defendant look guilty. The defense lawyers will try to make the jury see the witnesses as unreliable. The witnesses will testify one at a time, and the jury will decide whether each witness is truthful, untruthful, or neutral (giving a testimony that does not affect the case).

    a. Make a counting tree showing the combinations of ways that the jury might interpret the witnesses. Below is one way to begin the drawing.

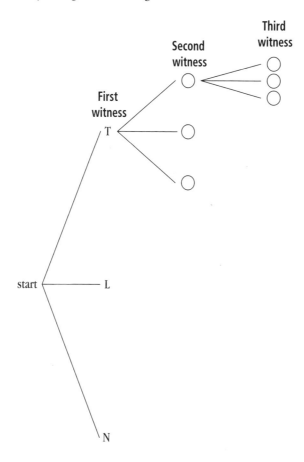

    b. The lawyers think that if the jury believes all three witnesses (truthful, truthful, truthful), they will probably convict the defendant. They might also convict the defendant if they believe only two of the three witnesses. List all the combinations that the lawyers think might lead to a conviction.

5. Chelsea has a collection of 82 shells.

    a. In how many ways could Chelsea select two shells? (Think about this: Is order important?)

    b. In how many ways could Chelsea select two shells if she wants one of the shells to be her pink cowry shell? Explain your reasoning.

    c. In how many ways could Chelsea select three shells from her collection?

    d. How many possibilities are there if one of the three shells selected is Chelsea's favorite snail shell?

© Dale Seymour Publications®

6. Morse code is a system in which letters, numbers, and punctuation marks are represented by sequences of dots and dashes. Each character is represented by at most five symbols. For example, *dot, dot, dot* represents the letter *s*. How many characters can be represented by sequences of at most five dots and dashes? Explain.

7. Suppose you invented a code in which combinations of the three symbols #, *, and % were used to represent the letters of the alphabet. In other words, a certain combination of these symbols represents the letter *A*, a certain combination represents the letter *B*, and so on. Each combination must contain the same number of symbols. How long a sequence would be needed to completely represent our alphabet? Explain.

8. A *palindrome* is a word that is spelled the same forward as it is backward, such as *tot* and *eye*. In this problem, a word is any combination of letters, whether it has meaning or not.

   a. How many three-letter palindromes are there with a consonant on each end and a vowel in the center?

   b. How many three-letter palindromes are there with a vowel at each end and a consonant in the center?

   c. How many different three-letter palindromes are there that are all vowels?

   d. How many different three-letter palindromes are there that are all consonants?

   e. How many different three-letter palindromes are there?

9. Alicia, a senior in high school, had a pre-graduation party with her friends Bes, Claudia, Delphy, and Elsa. After the party, Alicia plans to drive all her friends home and spend the night with the last person she takes home. It is a very hilly town. Alicia lives 3 miles from Bes, 1.5 miles from Claudia, 2 miles from Delphy, and 4 miles from Elsa. Bes lives 1 mile from Claudia, 3.5 miles from Delphy, and 2 miles from Elsa. Claudia lives 6 miles from Delphy and 4 miles from Elsa. Delphy lives 2 miles from Elsa. In what order should Alicia take her friends home, and with whom should she spend the night, if she wants to drive the shortest distance (including her drive home in the morning)?

10. a. Ziggy forgot the last two digits of his telephone number, but he remembers that they were both odd numbers. How many possibilities are there for him to try?

    b. If it takes Ziggy 15 seconds to dial a telephone number, how long will it take him to try each possibility?

11. a. Suppose Ziggy forgot the last two digits of his telephone number and couldn't remember whether they were odd or even. How many possibilities are there for him to try?

    b. If it takes Ziggy 15 seconds to dial a telephone number, how long will it take him to try each possibility?

12. A student traveling during the summer wants to visit the towns of Alba, Bica, Cinade, Delta, and Elta. Assume there is a road from each town to every other town. If the student begins from the train station, which is in none of these towns, how many different routes are possible for him to travel to visit each town?

© Dale Seymour Publications®

Unit Test

1. In the Three-to-Win lottery game, players choose three *different* numbers from 1 to 30. The order of the numbers matters, so the selection 4-22-6 is different from 6-4-22.

   a. How many possible lottery sequences are there?

   b. Tadashi plays the same sequence of numbers every week, 23-15-2. What is the probability that he will win this week?

   c. Are Tadashi's chances better because he plays the same sequence every week, or would they be better if he played a different sequence each week?

2. a. How many different dominoes are in a set of *double-four* dominoes, which have 0, 1, 2, 3, or 4 pips on each half? Explain how you found your answer.

   b. How many pips are in a complete set of double-four dominoes?

© Dale Seymour Publications®

3. Arlo, Batina, and Cie are standing in line at the theater. Draw a counting tree to show all the possible orders of first, second, and third in line.

4. To open this push-button lock, three *different* letters must be pressed in the correct order. How many possible combinations are there? Explain.

5. There are several routes for Denzell to ride his bike from his home to the sports center. Denzell says he can travel a different way every weekend for a year (52 weekends), never repeating the same journey. Is he correct? Explain.

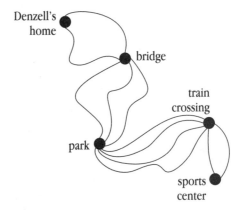

6. To log on to a computer network at the Idaho Institute of Engineering, you must enter a three-letter password. Sly remembers that his password contains three different vowels. He remembers which vowels, but he has forgotten their order. How many orders must he check?

© Dale Seymour Publications®

Unit Test

7. Ms. Callaway wants to choose a pair of students for a demonstration. She puts eight names into a box and draws two of them. The eight names are Alex, Bill, Carl, Darnel, Evelyn, Franny, Gloria, and Hannah.

   a. In how many ways can Ms. Callaway select a pair of students? Show how you found your answer.

   b. How many of the pairs consist of one name with four letters and one name with six letters? Show how you found your answer.

   c. Compare this problem to the problem of counting the number of different dominoes in a set. How are the problems similar? How are they different?

© Dale Seymour Publications®

Notebook Checklist

Journal Organization

_____ Problems and Mathematical Reflections are labeled and dated.

_____ Work is neat and is easy to find and follow.

Vocabulary

_____ All words are listed.   _____ All words are defined or described.

Check-Up and Quiz

_____ Check-Up

_____ Quiz

Homework Assignments

_____ _____

_____ _____

_____ _____

_____ _____

_____ _____

_____ _____

_____ _____

_____ _____

_____ _____

_____ _____

_____ _____

_____ _____

_____ _____

_____ _____

© Dale Seymour Publications®

Self-Assessment

Vocabulary

Of the vocabulary words I defined or described in my journal, the word _____ best demonstrates my ability to give a clear definition or description.

Of the vocabulary words I defined or described in my journal, the word _____ best demonstrates my ability to use an example to help explain or describe an idea.

Mathematical Ideas

1. a. In *Clever Counting*, I learned these things about . . .

   . . . situations in which multiplying is an appropriate counting strategy:

   . . . situations in which order is important and in which order is not important:

   . . . when *not* to use multiplication as a strategy for counting:

   b. Here are page numbers of journal entries that give evidence of what I have learned, along with descriptions of what each entry shows:

2. a. These are the mathematical ideas I am still struggling with:

   b. This is why I think these ideas are difficult for me:

   c. Here are page numbers of journal entries that give evidence of what I am struggling with, along with descriptions of what each entry shows:

Class Participation

I contributed to the classroom discussion and understanding of *Clever Counting* when I . . . (Give examples.)

© Dale Seymour Publications®

Answers to the Check-Up

1. **a.** There are 26 possible letters for each position, for $26 \times 26 \times 26 = 17{,}576$ sequences.

   b. There are 5 vowels and 21 consonants, so there are 21 choices for the first letter, 5 choices for the second, and only 1 choice for the third, or $21 \times 5 \times 1 = 105$ sequences.

2. **a.** Answers will vary, but there should be some evidence of organization for full credit. Possible answer:

1-0-2	1-2-0
1-0-3	1-2-3
1-0-4	1-2-4
1-0-5	1-2-5
1-0-6	1-2-6
1-0-7	1-2-7
1-0-8	1-2-8
1-0-9	1-2-9

   b. 10 ways

   c. 9 ways

   d. 8 ways

   e. $10 \times 9 \times 8 = 720$ combinations

3. There are 5 choices for the first button, 4 choices for the second button, and so on, for a total of $5 \times 4 \times 3 \times 2 \times 1 = 120$ sequences.

Answers to the Quiz

1. **a.** Possible answer:

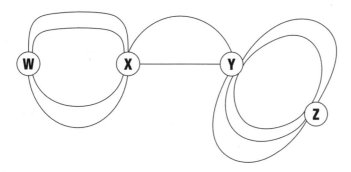

   b. In the above network, there are $4 \times 2 \times 5 = 40$ paths.

2. Possible answers:

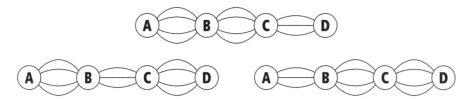

3. Possible answers:

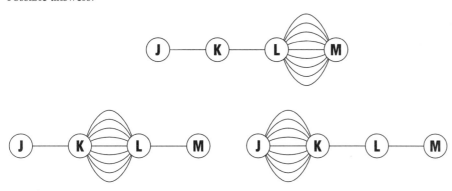

4. **a.** Nine buttons contain 3 letters each.

   b. $3 \times 3 \times 3 \times 3 = 81$ combinations

   c. Answers will vary. Some possibilities are EARN, FARM, and DARN.

3	2	7	6
D	(A)	P	M
(E)	B	(R)	(N)
F	C	S	O

5. There are 18 choices for the first site, 17 for the second, 16 for the third, and so on, or $18 \times 17 \times 16 \times 15 \times 14 \times 13 \times 12 \times \cdots \times 2 \times 1 \approx 6.4 \times 10^{15}$ orders. It would require $(6.4 \times 10^{15}) \times 2 \approx 1.28 \times 10^{16}$ minutes, or 2.13×10^{14} hours, or more than 24 billion years to trace them all! Obviously, listing and tracing all the possible orders is not a reasonable strategy.

Answers to the Question Bank

1. $3 \times 3 \times 3 = 27$ routes

2. **a.** $3 \times 2 \times 1 = 6$ ways

   b. $30 \times 29 \times 28 = 24{,}360$ selections

   c. $\frac{6}{24{,}360} = \frac{1}{4060}$

3. **a.** $10 \times 10 \times 10 = 1000$ tickets

   b. $500 \times \$3 = \$1500$ will be collected, which is exactly what is needed.

   c. Possible answer: There will not be enough tickets for all the students if more than 1000 want to buy a ticket. If fewer that 1000 tickets are purchased, it is possible that the winning numbers will not be purchased by anyone. The principal might have to continue drawing numbers until a winner is selected.

4. **a.**

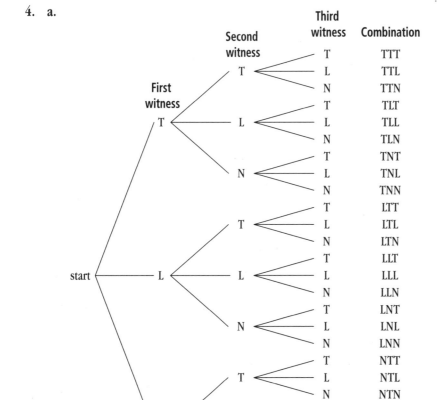

   b. TTT, TTL, TTN, TLT, TNT, LTT, NTT

5. **a.** $82 \times 81 = 6642$ ways

 b. 81 ways; Since one shell is already chosen, there are 81 shells left to choose from.

 c. $82 \times 81 \times 80 = 531,360$ ways

 d. $81 \times 80 = 6480$ ways

6. $2 + 2^2 + 2^3 + 2^4 + 2^5 = 2 + 4 + 8 + 16 + 32 = 62$ characters; A dot or a dash can be used in each position in sequences of length one, two, three, four, or five.

7. Since $3^3 = 27$, three-symbol sequences would completely represent our 26-letter alphabet.

8. **a.** $21 \times 5 \times 1 = 105$ palindromes

 b. $5 \times 21 \times 1 = 105$ palindromes

 c. $5 \times 5 \times 1 = 25$ palindromes

 d. $21 \times 21 \times 1 = 441$ palindromes

 e. $26 \times 26 \times 1 = 676$ palindromes

9. The best way to approach this problem is to draw a network and label the edges (this network is not drawn to scale). There is more than one shortest route. For example, A to D to E to B to C to A is 8.5 miles; Alicia will spend the night with Claudia. A to C to B to E to D to A is also 8.5 miles, and she will spend the night with Delphy.

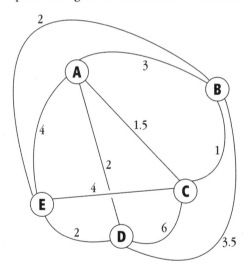

10. **a.** $5 \times 5 = 25$ possibilities

 b. $25 \times 15 = 375$ seconds, or 6.25 minutes

11. **a.** $10 \times 10 = 100$ possibilities

 b. $100 \times 15 = 1500$ seconds, or 25 minutes

12. $5 \times 4 \times 3 \times 2 \times 1 = 120$ routes

Answers to the Unit Test

1. **a.** $30 \times 29 \times 28 = 24{,}360$ sequences

    b. $\frac{1}{24{,}360}$

    c. His chances are the same no matter what sequence he plays each week. The chance of any single sequence coming up on any particular week is $\frac{1}{24{,}360}$.

2. **a.** There are 15 dominoes: 0-0, 0-1, 0-2, 0-3, 0-4, 1-1, 1-2, 1-3, 1-4, 2-2, 2-3, 2-4, 3-3, 3-4, and 4-4.

    b. Each number appears 6 times, so there are $6(0 + 1 + 2 + 3 + 4) = 60$ pips.

3.

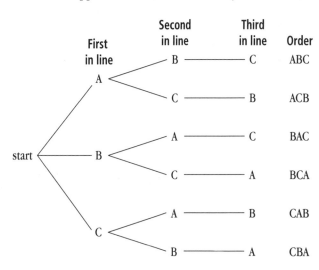

4. There are 5 choices for the first button, 4 for the second, and 3 for the third, for $5 \times 4 \times 3 = 60$ combinations.

5. There are 2 ways from Denzell's home to the bridge, 3 ways from the bridge to the park, 4 ways from the park to the train crossing, and 2 ways from the train crossing to the sports center, for $2 \times 3 \times 4 \times 2 = 48$ routes, not quite enough to travel a different way each weekend.

6. Sly remembers which three vowels, so he has 3 choices for the first vowel, 2 for the second, and 1 for the third, for a total of $3 \times 2 \times 1 = 6$ orders.

7. **a.** 28 ways; Strategies will vary. Some students may make a list: AB, AC, AD, AE, AF, AG, AH, BC, BD, BE, BF, BG, BH, CD, CE, CF, CG, CH, DE, DF, DG, DH, EF, EG, EH, FG, FH, GH. Some may make a diagram. Some may reason that there are 8 ways to choose the first person and 7 ways to choose the second. This is a total of $8 \times 7 = 56$ pairs, but AB is the same as BA, so there are really only 28 pairs.

    b. Strategies will vary. There are 15 such pairs: AD, AE, AF, AG, AH, BD, BE, BF, BG, BH, CD, CE, CF, CG, CH, or $3 \times 5 = 15$.

    c. In the domino problem, numbers of pips are paired, as names are paired in this problem. Also, order does not matter in either problem, so one has to be careful not to count dominoes or student pairs twice. The problems are different in that doubles are allowed in the domino problem but not in the student-pair problem.

The optional unit project consists of two separate projects. They provide an opportunity for students to apply their understanding of ways to count situations, combinations, and the like.

Project 1: Writing a Detective Story

In this project, students apply what they have learned about counting to write their own mystery stories that incorporate various kinds of counting situations. To write their stories, students will draw from the ideas they have recorded after each set of Mathematical Reflections questions.

Discuss the project with students before assigning it, and develop with them the guidelines for what will constitute an excellent, good, passing, or inadequate paper. Below are examples of guidelines you might include.

Excellent	Good	Passing	Inadequate
Story shows how the number of possible combinations is a crucial clue.	Story shows how the number of possible combinations is a crucial clue.	Story shows how the number of possible combinations is a crucial clue.	Story does not show how the number of possible combinations is a crucial clue.
There are at least 4 clues that involve counting combinations (routes, codes, license plates, partial names or numbers left on crumpled notes, possible conspirators?).	There are at least 3 clues that involve counting combinations.	There are at least 2 clues that involve counting combinations.	There is only 1 or there are no clues that involve counting combinations.
Calculations are done correctly.	Calculations contain only minor mistakes.	Calculations are partially correct.	Errors in calculations indicate lack of understanding.
The rate at which something can be made, done, or checked (such as the rate at which roads are blocked or telephone numbers are traced) is an important clue and is correctly calculated.	The rate at which something can be made, done, or checked features as an important clue; its calculation contains minor errors.	The rate at which something can be made, done, or checked is a clue but is not well explained.	Rate is not featured in the story.
Clear explanations are given by the detective, and the paper shows a good use of vocabulary, grammar, graphs, grids, and diagrams as necessary.	Explanations are fairly clear, but the written language or graphics could be improved.	Explanations and diagrams are attempted, but are not clear.	Explanations are not clear, and diagrams were not attempted or are not understandable.

Project 2: Making Trains

In this project, students apply their knowledge of searching for patterns and writing equations to what they have learned about counting. Students will need a copy of Labsheet UP, which contains a set of rectangles. Each rectangle represents a "car" that will be put together to make "trains." A train may consist of a single car. The labsheet contains the following cars:

10-car

9-car

8-car

7-car

6-car

5-car

4-car

3-car

2-car

1-car

The train project can also be investigated with Cuisenaire rods, if they are available, which are made in integer lengths from 1 centimeter to 10 centimeters. The colors of the rods may help some students to see patterns.

Exploring the Project

Students will cut out the rectangles from the labsheet (or work with a set of Cuisenaire rods in the same lengths) to investigate making trains. For each car length, they are to look for trains of the same length. A *train* is defined as a single car or two or more cars placed end-to-end, and order is important. For example, four trains can be made equal in length to the 3-car: three 1-cars, a 1-car followed by a 2-car, a 2-car followed by a 1-car, and a 3-car.

Students record the length of each car and the number of trains that can be made of that length. From the pattern they see in their results, they write an equation for the relationship between the length of a car, L, and the number of trains with that length, N. They are also asked to compare the pattern they discover with patterns they have seen in other situations in *Clever Counting*.

Ask students to give both specific examples and general arguments to justify their conclusions. They may want to include sketches in the body of their papers or attach separate pages of figures.

A table of the overall relationships is given below. An equation modeling this relationship is $N = 2^{L-1}$, where L is length of a car and N is the number of trains of this length.

Car length (cm)	1	2	3	4	5	6	7	8	9	10
Trains of this length	1	2	4	8	16	32	64	128	256	512

Suggested Scoring Rubric

One way to assess this project is to assign it 50 points, distributed as follows:

35 points for content and substance
How many patterns has the student found? Are explanations correct and complete? Has the student showed connections to the course?

10 points for style and mechanics
Is the paper well organized? Are spelling and punctuation appropriate?

5 points for creativity, effort, and quality
Is this an exceptional paper? Does it go beyond the project requirements in some unique way?

The first assessment piece for *Clever Counting* is the check-up. A suggested scoring rubric and grading scale for the check-up are presented here.

Suggested Scoring Rubric

This rubric employs a scale with a total of 18 possible points. You may use the rubric as presented here or modify it to fit your district's requirements for evaluating and reporting students' work and understanding.

question 1: 6 points

- *part a:* 1 point for determining the correct number of sequences and 2 points for an explanation that shows understanding of the mathematics concepts and tells how the solution was found (1 point for a partial explanation that shows some understanding)
- *part b:* 1 point for the correct solution and 2 points for an explanation that shows understanding of the mathematics concepts and tells how the solution was found (1 point for a partial explanation that shows some understanding)

question 2: 7 points

- *part a:* 1 point for a correct list
- *part b:* 1 point for a correct solution
- *part c:* 1 point for a correct solution
- *part d:* 1 point for a correct solution
- *part e:* 1 point for a correct solution

question 3: 5 points

- 2 points for a correct solution (1 point for a solution that shows some understanding.)
- 3 points for a complete explanation that shows understanding of the mathematics (2 points for a partial explanation that shows some understanding; 1 point for an insufficient explanation that shows minimal understanding)

Grading Scale

Points	Grade
16 to 18	A
14 to 15	B
11 to 13	C
9 to 10	D

The second assessment piece for *Clever Counting* is the partner quiz. A suggested scoring rubric and grading scale for the quiz are presented here.

Suggested Scoring Rubric

This rubric employs a scale with a total of 14 possible points. You may use the rubric as presented here or modify it to fit your district's requirements for evaluating and reporting students' work and understanding.

question 1: 3 points
- *part a:* 2 points for a network that satisfies the essential conditions of the problem (1 point for a network that satisfies some of the essential conditions)
- *part b:* 1 point for a correct solution

question 2: 2 points
- 2 points for a correct network that has 11 edges and the maximum number of paths (1 point for a network with 11 edges and close to the maximum number of paths)

question 3: 2 points
- 2 points for a correct network that has 11 edges and the minimum number of paths (1 point for a network with 11 edges and close to the minimum number of paths)

question 4: 4 points
- *part a:* 1 point for a correct solution
- *part b:* 2 points for a correct solution (1 point for an incorrect solution that shows some understanding of the mathematics necessary to solve the problem)
- *part c:* 1 point for a correct solution

question 5: 3 points
- 3 points for a complete explanation that shows understanding of the mathematics (2 points for a partial explanation that shows some understanding; 1 point for an insufficient explanation that shows minimal understanding of the mathematics)

Grading Scale

Points	Grade
13 to 14	A
11 to 12	B
9 to 10	C
7 to 8	D

Blackline Masters

Making Trains

10-car

9-car

9-car

8-car	8-car

8-car	8-car

7-car	7-car

7-car	7-car

6-car	6-car

6-car	6-car

5-car	5-car	5-car

5-car	5-car	5-car

4-car	4-car	4-car	4-car

4-car	4-car	4-car	4-car

3-car	3-car	3-car	3-car	3-car

3-car	3-car	3-car	3-car	3-car

2-car	2-car	2-car	2-car	2-car	2-car	2-car

2-car	2-car	2-car	2-car	2-car	2-car	2-car

1-car	1-car	1-car	1-car	1-car	1-car	1-car	1-car	1-car	1-car	1-car	1-car

1-car	1-car	1-car	1-car	1-car	1-car	1-car	1-car	1-car	1-car	1-car	1-car

© Dale Seymour Publications®

Here are the choices the artist gave the witness:

Hair	**Eyes**	**Nose**
bushy	staring	hooked
bald	beady	long and straight
	droopy	turned up
	wide open	broken

A. How many facial descriptions can you make by choosing one attribute for each feature?

B. The witness said he remembered something distinctive about the driver's mouth. The artist suggested these possibilities:

Mouth
thin and mean
toothless
sinister grin

If you consider the hair, eyes, nose, and mouth, how many facial descriptions can you make by choosing one attribute for each feature?

© Dale Seymour Publications®

The witness claimed that he saw the license plate of the van. In the state in which the robbery took place, license plates contain three letters followed by three numbers. He said that it was an in-state plate containing the letters MTU.

Detective Curious wants to run each possible plate number through the computer to find out whether the registered owner has a criminal record. It takes about 20 seconds to check each plate number.

How many possible plates start with MTU?

Do you think this is a reasonable number of plates for the detective to check?

© Dale Seymour Publications®

A lock sequence may have two, three, four, or five letters. A letter may not occur more than once in a sequence.

A. How many two-letter sequences are possible?

B. How many three-letter sequences are possible?

C. How many four-letter sequences are possible?

D. How many five-letter sequences are possible?

E. The security guard would not have known whether the sequence that would open Rodney's lock consisted of two, three, four, or five letters. How many possible lock sequences might she have had to try?

© Dale Seymour Publications®

A. How many possible combinations are there for Rodney's lock? Assume that a number may not appear more than once in a combination.

B. How long do you think it would take someone to try all the possible combinations? Explain how you made your estimate.

© Dale Seymour Publications®

A. Make a table showing the number of possible combinations for locks with from 3 to 10 marks. Consider only three-number combinations with no repeated numbers. For example, to complete the row for 3 marks, consider all possible combinations of the numbers 0, 1, and 2.

Number of marks	Number of combinations
3	
4	
5	
6	
7	
8	
9	
10	

B. Use the pattern in your table to write an equation for the relationship between the number of marks, m, and the number of combinations, C.

C. Sketch a graph of your equation for m values from 3 to 10.

D. How could the manager use your graph to convince the owner to buy locks with more marks?

© Dale Seymour Publications®

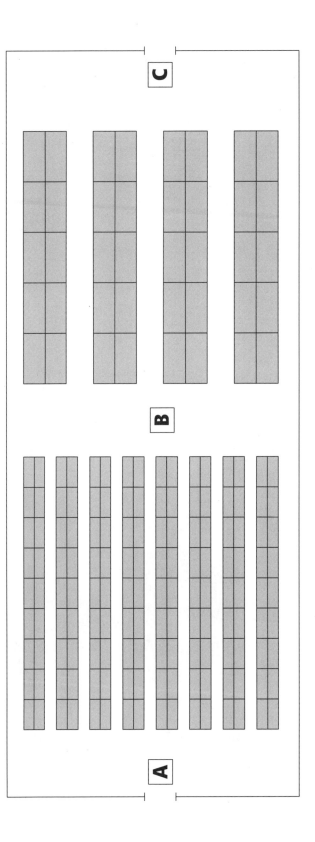

© Dale Seymour Publications®

A. How many paths are there from A to B? How many paths are there from B to C?

B. How many paths are there from A to C through B? Explain your reasoning.

C. If Rodney has a small locker, how many of the paths from A to C pass by his locker?

D. If Rodney has a large locker, how many of the paths from A to C pass by his locker?

E. If Rodney has a small locker, what is the probability that the guard will *not* pass his locker on one of her rounds?

F. If Rodney has a large locker, what is the probability that the guard will *not* pass his locker on one of her rounds?

© Dale Seymour Publications®

A. In this network, a single edge connects node A to node B, and 8 edges connect node B to node C. How many paths are there from node A to node C that pass through node B?

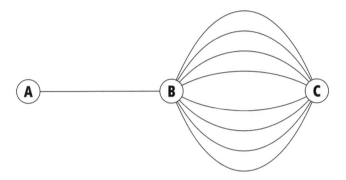

B. In this network, 2 edges connect node A to node B, and 5 edges connect node B to node C. How many paths are there from node A to node C that pass through node B?

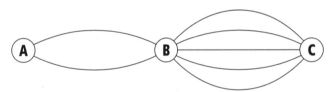

C. In another network, 25 edges connect node A to node B, and 32 edges connect node B to node C. How many paths are there from node A to node C that pass through node B? Explain your reasoning.

© Dale Seymour Publications®

A. 1. Design at least three networks with nodes A, B, and C and 12 edges. Each edge should connect node A to node B or node B to node C.

2. For each network you drew, record the number of edges from node A to node B, the number of edges from node B to node C, and the total number of paths from node A to node C. Look for a pattern in your results.

3. Use your findings from part 2 to help you draw the network with the maximum number of paths from node A to node C. Explain how you know that your network has the maximum number of paths.

© Dale Seymour Publications®

B. Design a network with nodes A, B, C, and D and 12 edges that has the maximum number of paths from node A to node D through nodes B and C. How did you decide how to distribute the 12 edges?

C. Suppose you are given a specific number of nodes and a specific number of edges. How can you design a network with the maximum number of paths from the first node to the last node?

D. Describe how the numbers of edges between consecutive pairs of nodes are related to the total number of paths in a network.

© Dale Seymour Publications®

 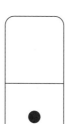    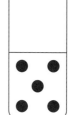

 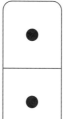 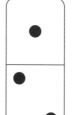 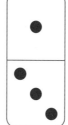 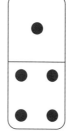 

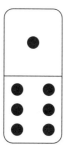 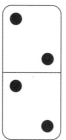 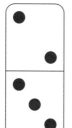 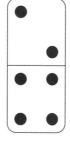  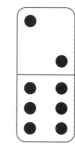

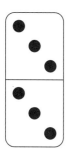 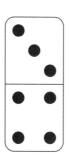 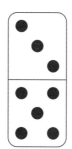 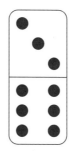 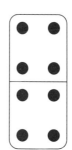 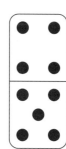

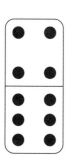 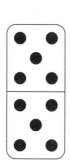 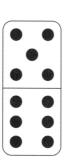 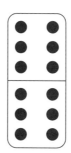

© Dale Seymour Publications®

A. How many different dominoes are in a complete set?

B. The vending machines at Fail-Safe offer seven types of sandwiches and seven different drinks. The security guard wants to buy one sandwich and one drink. From how many combinations can she choose?

C. The security guard in a nearby storage warehouse can follow seven routes from checkpoint A to checkpoint B and seven routes from checkpoint B to checkpoint C. How many routes can he follow from checkpoint A to checkpoint C through checkpoint B?

D. Parts A–C each involve finding the number of ways to fill two positions when there are seven choices for each position. Compare the strategies you used to answer each part. How are the strategies similar? How are they different?

© Dale Seymour Publications®

The manager narrowed his choices to six models: the ACME CrimeStopper, the BurgleProof 2000, the Citadel, the Deterrent, the EverSafe, and the Fortress. He chose two locks to bring to the meeting.

A. There are several ways the manager could have chosen the two locks. In how many different ways could the manager have chosen the two locks? Prove your answer is correct by listing all the possible pairs of locks.

B. If the manager had taken three locks to the meeting, in how many different ways could he have chosen them? Prove your answer is correct by listing all the possible sets of three locks.

C. How is finding the number of different ways the manager could have chosen the locks similar to and different from finding the number of lock combinations in Investigation 2?

© Dale Seymour Publications®

You know as much as the detective does about counting combinations and calculating probabilities. Imagine that the detective asks you to help her with the case.

A. Which pieces of evidence would you investigate further? How would you proceed with your investigation?

B. What questions would you ask the security guard, the manager, or someone else involved in the case?

C. Does the evidence from the second robbery clear any of the suspects? Who are your suspects now? Why?

© Dale Seymour Publications®

Dear Family,

The last unit in your child's course of study in mathematics class this year involves one of the most common aspects of arithmetic that we encountered as young children, but that can become complicated very quickly: counting.

When we learned to count, we probably memorized the numbers 1, 2, 3, and so on. Only later did we understand what those words meant. In their mathematics work this year, students have had many opportunities to further their understanding of numbers and operations. In *Clever Counting,* they learn to recognize situations in which multiplication can help them to count how many ways certain events can happen. As students work on the unit, they will increase their skill with multiplication and making sense of large numbers.

The task of counting becomes complicated when we place conditions on what we are counting. Students will investigate a fictitious robbery in this unit. In the process, they will be asked to count, among other things, the number of combinations a lock can have, the number of license plates that are possible with particular characteristics, and the number of paths a night guard might travel during periodic inspection rounds.

Here are some strategies for helping your child during this unit:

- Ask for an explanation of the ideas about counting that are presented in the book.

- Help your child locate examples of counting that people deal with in their everyday lives.

- Discuss with your child real situations in which counting techniques are used; for example, the field of cryptoanalysis, a branch of mathematics in which people work with secret codes such as those used in banks and most businesses.

- Encourage your child to do his or her homework every day. Look over the homework and make sure all questions are answered and that explanations are clear.

As always, if you have any questions or suggestions about your child's mathematics program, please feel free to call.

Sincerely,

© Dale Seymour Publications®

Estimada familia,

La última unidad del programa de matemáticas de su hijo o hija para este curso trata sobre uno de los aspectos de la aritmética que cuando fuimos niños más comúnmente utilizamos y que puede llegar a complicarse con suma facilidad: el contar.

Cuando aprendimos a contar, probablemente lo hicimos memorizando los números 1, 2, 3 y así sucesivamente. Y fue en algún momento posterior cuando realmente llegamos a entender lo que significaban esas palabras. En el trabajo matemático que los alumnos han realizado este año han tenido muchas oportunidades para aumentar sus conocimientos acerca de los números y las operaciones. En *Clever Counting* (Contar inteligentemente), aprenden a identificar situaciones en las que la multiplicación les puede ayudar a contar la cantidad de maneras en que pueden ocurrir ciertos sucesos. Durante el estudio de esta unidad, perfeccionarán sus destrezas relacionadas con la multiplicación y con la comprensión de las grandes cifras.

El contar puede llegar a ser complicado cuando imponemos condiciones al objeto que contamos. En esta unidad los alumnos examinarán un robo ficticio y, como parte de dicho proceso, se les pedirá que cuenten, entre otras cosas, el número de combinaciones que puede tener una cerradura, el número de placas de matrícula que puede haber con ciertas características y el número de caminos diferentes que un guarda nocturno puede recorrer durante sus rondas periódicas de vigilancia.

Aparecen a continuación algunas estrategias que ustedes pueden emplear para ayudar a su hijo o hija en esta unidad:

- Pídanle que les explique las ideas relativas al conteo que se presentan en el libro.

- Ayúdenle a buscar ejemplos en la vida diaria en los que la gente tenga que contar.

- Comenten juntos situaciones reales en las que se emplean técnicas de conteo. Un ejemplo puede ser el campo del criptoanálisis, una rama de las matemáticas en la que se manejan códigos secretos, como los utilizados en los bancos y en la mayoría de los negocios.

- Anímenle a hacer la tarea todos los días. Repásenla para asegurarse de que conteste todas las preguntas y escriba con claridad las explicaciones.

Y como de costumbre, si ustedes tienen alguna duda o recomendación relacionada con el programa de matemáticas de su hijo o hija, no duden en llamarnos.

Atentamente,

© Dale Seymour Publications®

Additional Practice

Investigation 1

Use these problems for additional practice after Investigation 1.

Three buckets each contain four balls marked with a letter or a number.

Bucket I   Bucket II   Bucket III

1. Suppose one ball is drawn from bucket I and one ball is drawn from bucket II. Make a counting tree to show how many different combinations of characters—letters or numbers—are possible.

2. Suppose one ball is drawn from bucket II and one ball is drawn from bucket III. How many different combinations of characters are possible? Explain your reasoning.

3. Suppose one ball is drawn from bucket I and one ball is drawn from bucket III. How many different combinations of characters are possible? Explain your reasoning.

4. Suppose one ball is drawn from each bucket. How many possible combinations contain *only* numbers? Explain your reasoning.

5. Suppose one ball is drawn from each bucket. How many possible combinations contain *only* letters? Explain your reasoning.

6. Suppose one ball is drawn from each bucket. How many possible combinations *do not* contain consonants or odd numbers? Explain your reasoning.

Use this information to answer 7–9: In one state, license plates contain three letters followed by four numbers. The letters I, O, and Q are not used because they might be mistaken for the numbers 1 or 0.

7. How many different plates could be made using this system? Explain your reasoning.

8. How many cars in this state can have plates in which all the letters are vowels (A, E, I, O, or U)? Explain your reasoning.

9. How many cars in this state can have plates in which all the digits are odd? Explain your reasoning.

© Dale Seymour Publications®

10. Telephone numbers consist of a three-digit *prefix* followed by a four-digit number, such as 555-2870. Suppose the numbers 0, 1, 2, 3, 4, 5, 6, 7, 8, 9 can be used for each digit. How many local telephone numbers are possible? Explain your reasoning.

In North America, telephone numbers consist of a three-digit *area code,* followed by a three-digit *prefix,* followed by four more digits. In the telephone number (517) 555-2870, 517 is the area code. In 11–14, assume that the digits from 0 to 9 can be used in any location in a phone number.

11. In a state with 4 area codes, how many telephone numbers are possible? Explain your reasoning.

12. In a state with 12 area codes, how many telephone numbers are possible?

13. In a state with 8 area codes, how many telephone numbers are possible?

14. Suppose a state is running out of telephone numbers and anticipates the need for 10 million new telephone numbers over the next five years. How many new area codes will the state need to meet this increase? Explain your reasoning.

The Metropolis school district has an enrollment of 26,479 students. The district wants to assign an identification code to each student.

15. Suppose you are in charge of developing an ID system. Describe a system that would provide enough ID codes for all the students and require the fewest characters (letters or numbers). Explain your reasoning.

16. Suppose the ID codes cannot contain letters. Describe an ID system that would provide enough ID codes and require the fewest characters. Explain your answer.

17. Are your answers to 16 and 17 different? Explain why they are the same or different.

© Dale Seymour Publications®

Investigation 2

Use these problems for additional practice after Investigation 2.

In 1–6, consider any combination of letters a "word," even if you can't pronounce the word and have no idea whether it has any meaning.

1. How many three-letter words can be made with the letters X, Y, and Z if letters *can* be repeated?

2. How many three-letter words can be made with the letters X, Y, and Z if letters *cannot* be repeated?

3. How many three-letter words can be made with the letters Q, R, X, Y, and Z if letters *can* be repeated?

4. How many three-letter words can be made with the letters Q, R, X, Y, and Z if letters *cannot* be repeated?

5. How many *three-letter* words can be made with the letters X and L with repeats allowed?

6. How many *five-letter* words can be made with the letters X and L with repeats allowed?

In 7–9, use this information: Felix and Emily are decorating the school gym for the spring dance. They decide to string balloons in a repeating pattern of four balloons. They have six different colors of balloons to choose from.

7. If the four balloons in the pattern will each be a different color, how many patterns are possible? Explain how you found your answer.

8. Suppose Felix and Emily eliminate the two colors that are the least bright. If the four balloons in the pattern will each be a different color, how many patterns are possible?

9. If Emily and Felix decide to use only four colors, but make the pattern five balloons long with one color repeated, how many patterns are possible? Explain how you found your answer.

© Dale Seymour Publications®

10. The science club is holding a raffle to raise money for new laboratory equipment. The raffle tickets contain four characters. The first character can be any letter of the alphabet. Each of the three remaining characters can be any number from 0 to 9. To win, a raffle ticket must match a randomly generated string exactly.

a. How many tickets are possible that begin with the letter K?

b. How many tickets are possible that end with two zeros?

c. Kathy, the treasurer of the science club, says that she has just realized that since there are 1150 students and 50 teachers at the school, it is likely that even if every student and teacher bought a raffle ticket, no one would have a winning ticket.

   i. Do you agree with Kathy? Explain why or why not.

   ii. Assuming that every raffle ticket is different, how many raffle tickets would each student and teacher have to buy to guarantee that someone would have the winning ticket? Explain your answer.

d. Based on your answer to part c, would you change the character string on the raffle tickets? If so, describe a new character string and why it would be better. If not, explain why you would leave the string unchanged.

11. In one state, license plates contain three letters followed by four numbers. The letters I, O, and Q are not used because they might be mistaken for the numbers 1 or 0. How many different plates could be made in this state if no letters or numbers can be repeated? Explain your reasoning.

12. There are eight Connected Mathematics units for grade 8.

a. In how many different sequences can the eight units be arranged on a bookshelf?

b. In how many different sequences can the eight units be arranged on a bookshelf if *Clever Counting* is the last unit in the sequence?

© Dale Seymour Publications

Investigation 3

Use these problems for additional practice after Investigation 3.

Use the network below to answer questions 1–5.

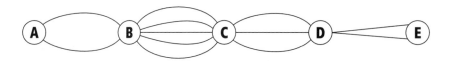

1. How many nodes does the network have?

2. How many edges does the network have?

3. How many paths are there from node B to node D?

4. How many paths are there from node B to node E?

5. How many paths are there from node A to node E?

6. a. The network below represents the highways connecting four cities. How many highway routes are there from city W to city Z that pass through cities X and Y?

   b. How many different highway round trips are there from city W to city Z and back to city W?

   c. Suppose one of the highways from city X to city Y is closed due to road construction. How does that change the number of highway routes from city W to city Z through cities X and Y?

7. Design a network with nodes A, B, C, and D and exactly 15 edges that has the maximum number of paths from node A to node D through nodes B and C. How many paths does your network have?

8. Design a network with nodes E, F, G, and H so that there are exactly 27 paths from node E to node H passing through nodes F and G.

© Dale Seymour Publications®

9. Design a network with nodes A, B, C, D, E, and F so that there are exactly 32 paths from node A to node F passing through nodes B, C, D, and E.

10. Design a network with nodes Z, ZZ, and ZZZ so that there are exactly 3 paths from node Z to node ZZZ passing through node ZZ.

11. J, K, L, and M are the corners of a square. There is one direct path between each pair of corners. How many paths are there from J through each of the other three points and back to J? Explain.

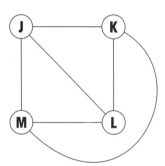

© Dale Seymour Publications

Investigation 4

Use these problems for additional practice after Investigation 4.

1. How many different dominoes are in a set of *double-three* dominoes, which have from 0 to 3 pips on each half? Explain how you found your answer.

2. How many different dominoes are in a set of *double-seven* dominoes, which have from 0 to 7 pips on each half? Explain how you found your answer.

3. How many pips in all are in a set of *double-three* dominoes? Explain.

4. How many pips in all are in a set of *double-seven* dominoes? Explain.

5. In the card game Mix and Match, players can trade in sets of three cards for extra points. There are three different cards in the game, each with a different pattern.

     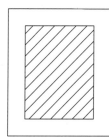 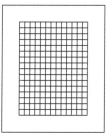

    To trade in a set of three cards, a player must have three of one card (three alike) or one of each card (all different).

    a. How many different possible sets of three trade-in cards are there? Explain.

    b. Narciso claims that if you have five cards, you must be able to make a set to trade in for extra points. Do you agree with Narciso? Explain why or why not.

6. In how many different ways can three bows be chosen from a bag of four bows?

7. In how many different ways can three bows be chosen from a bag of six bows?

© Dale Seymour Publications®

Investigation 5

Use these problems for additional practice after Investigation 5.

1. The computer in the children's library requires users to have a password consisting of two characters, such as Z9. Each character may be any letter or any digit, but no letter or digit can be repeated in the password.

    a. How many passwords are possible?

    b. How many more passwords could be used if repeating letters or digits were allowed? Explain your answer.

2. The local cafe sells ice cream sundaes that include 2 toppings. There are 12 toppings to choose from. How many combinations of two *different* toppings are possible?

3. The Megalopolis computer system requires users to have a password that contains at least four characters and no more than six characters, such as A1744K and A174. A character can be either a letter or a number, and letters and numbers may be repeated in a password.

    a. How many passwords are possible on this system? Show how you found your answer.

    b. Suppose a computer hacker tries to break into the system. The hacker writes a program that can generate and test 10^6 passwords of four to six characters per second. At this rate, how long would it take the hacker to test every possible password?

4. Many people who use automated teller machine (ATM) cards for banking must remember a four-digit personal identification number (PIN).

    a. If each digit in a four-digit PIN is a number from 0 to 9, how many possible four-digit PINs are there?

    b. A large bank has 76,500 customers who have ATM cards. Each of these cards has a four-digit PIN. Do you think that some customers have the same PIN? Why or why not?

Investigation 1

1. 16 combinations are possible.

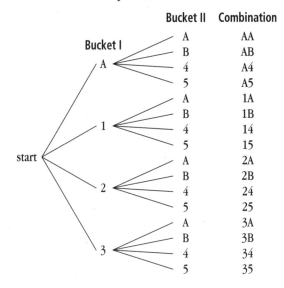

	Bucket II	Combination
	A	AA
	B	AB
A	4	A4
	5	A5
	A	1A
	B	1B
1	4	14
	5	15
	A	2A
	B	2B
2	4	24
	5	25
	A	3A
	B	3B
3	4	34
	5	35

2. $4 \times 4 = 16$ combinations; There are 4 balls in each bucket.

3. $4 \times 4 = 16$ combinations; There are 4 balls in each bucket.

4. $3 \times 2 \times 2 = 12$ combinations; Multiply the number of balls containing only numbers.

5. $1 \times 2 \times 2 = 4$ combinations; Multiply the number of balls containing only letters.

6. $2 \times 2 \times 3 = 12$ combinations; Multiply the number of balls containing only vowels or even numbers.

7. $23 \times 23 \times 23 \times 10 \times 10 \times 10 \times 10 = 121{,}670{,}000$ plates; There are 23 letters available for each of the first three positions.

8. $5 \times 5 \times 5 \times 10 \times 10 \times 10 \times 10 = 1{,}250{,}000$ plates; There are 5 letters available for each of the last four positions.

9. $23 \times 23 \times 23 \times 5 \times 5 \times 5 \times 5 = 7{,}604{,}375$ plates; There are 5 numbers (1, 3, 5, 7, 9) available for each of the last four positions.

10. $10^7 = 10{,}000{,}000$; Each of the seven digits can be one of 10 numbers under this assumption.

11. $4 \times 10^7 = 40{,}000{,}000$; There are 10^7 local telephone numbers for each area code.

12. $12 \times 10^7 = 120{,}000{,}000$; There are 10^7 local telephone numbers for each area code.

13. $8 \times 10^7 = 80{,}000{,}000$; There are 10^7 local telephone numbers for each area code.

14. The state will need one new area code, which will supply $10^7 = 10{,}000{,}000$ new numbers.

15. Possible answer: If a character can be a letter or a number, a three-character ID code would provide $36^3 = 46{,}656$ ID numbers.

16. A five-digit code would provide $10^5 = 100{,}000$ possible codes (a four-digit code would supply only $10^4 = 10{,}000$ codes).

17. Possible answer: They are different because allowing characters to be letters or numbers gives 36 possibilities per character instead of only 10.

Answer Keys

Investigation 2

1. $3 \times 3 \times 3 = 27$ words

2. $3 \times 2 \times 1 = 6$ words

3. $5 \times 5 \times 5 = 125$ words

4. $5 \times 4 \times 3 = 60$ words

5. $2 \times 2 \times 2 = 8$ words

6. $2 \times 2 \times 2 \times 2 \times 2 = 32$ words

7. $6 \times 5 \times 4 \times 3 = 360$ patterns; There are 6 color choices for the first balloon in the pattern, 5 color choices for the second, 4 color choices for the third, and 3 color choices for the fourth.

8. $4 \times 3 \times 2 \times 1 = 24$ patterns

9. $4 \times 3 \times 2 \times 1 \times 4 = 96$ patterns; There are 4 color choices for the first balloon in the pattern, 3 color choices for the second, 2 color choices for the third, 1 color choice for the fourth, and 4 color choices for the fifth (this is the repeated color).

10.   a. $10 \times 10 \times 10 = 1000$ tickets

    b. $26 \times 10 = 260$ tickets

    c. i. There are $26 \times 10 \times 10 \times 10 = 26{,}000$ possible tickets. If only 1200 tickets are purchased, there is only about a 4.6% chance that someone will have the winning ticket.

       ii. Each student and teacher would have to buy 21 or 22 tickets to guarantee that the randomly selected string would match one of the tickets.

    d. Answers will vary. Students might suggest, for example, using a three-digit string and selling all 1000 tickets to the 1200 students or selecting the winning ticket number from among the tickets sold.

11. $23 \times 22 \times 21 \times 10 \times 9 \times 8 \times 7 = 53{,}555{,}040$ plates; There are 23 choices available for the first position, 22 for the second, 21 for the third, 10 for the fourth, 9 for the fifth, 8 for the sixth, and 7 for the seventh.

12.   a. $8 \times 7 \times 6 \times 5 \times 4 \times 3 \times 2 \times 1 = 40{,}320$ sequences

    b. $7 \times 6 \times 5 \times 4 \times 3 \times 2 \times 1 = 5040$ sequences

Investigation 3

1. 5 nodes

2. $2 + 5 + 3 + 2 = 12$ edges

3. $5 \times 3 = 15$ paths

4. $5 \times 3 \times 2 = 30$ paths

5. $2 \times 5 \times 3 \times 2 = 60$ paths

6.   a. $3 \times 5 \times 4 = 60$ highway routes

    b. $60 \times 60 = 3600$ round trips

    c. There are now $3 \times 4 \times 4 = 48$ routes, 12 fewer routes, or 0.8 times as many routes, as when all the highways are open.

7. There are $5 \times 5 \times 5 = 125$ paths from node A to node C through node B.

8. Answers will vary. Possible answers:

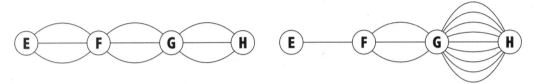

9. Answers will vary. Possible answers:

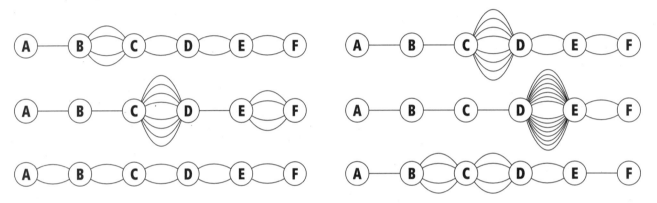

10. Possible answers:

11. Think of this as a choices problem. Starting from J, there are three choices for the first point to visit, two choices for the second, and one choice for the third; a total of $3 \times 2 \times 1 = 6$ paths. The paths are JKLMJ, JKMLJ, JLKMJ, JLMKJ, JMKLJ, and JMLKJ.

Investigation 4

1. There are 10 different dominoes. One solution method is to make a list:

0-0	0-1	0-2	0-3
	1-1	1-2	1-3
		2-2	2-3
			3-3

2. There are 36 different dominoes. One solution method is to make a list:

0-0	0-1	0-2	0-3	0-4	0-5	0-6	0-7
	1-1	1-2	1-3	1-4	1-5	1-6	1-7
		2-2	2-3	2-4	2-5	2-6	2-7
			3-3	3-4	3-5	3-6	3-7
				4-4	4-5	4-6	4-7
					5-5	5-6	5-7
						6-6	6-7
							7-7

3. Each number appears 5 times, so there are $5(0 + 1 + 2 + 3) = 30$ pips.

4. Each number appears 9 times, so there are $9(0 + 1 + 2 + 3 + 4 + 5 + 6 + 7) = 252$ pips.

5. **a.** There are four sets: three sets containing three of a pattern and one set containing one of each pattern.

    b. Yes, five cards guarantee a trade-in set. With four cards, a player must be holding two pairs. Drawing a fifth card, no matter what it is, the player will either complete three of a kind or have a set containing one of each.

6. 4 ways; Suppose the bows are lettered A, B, C, and D. Four sets of three are possible because order doesn't matter: ABC, ABD, ACD, and BCD.

7. 20 ways; Suppose the bows are lettered A, B, C, D, E, and F. Twenty sets of three are possible because order doesn't matter: ABC, ABD, ABE, ABF, ACD, ACE, ACF, ADE, ADF, AEF, BCD, BCE, BCF, BDE, BDF, BEF, CDE, CDF, CEF, and DEF.

Investigation 5

1. **a.** $36 \times 35 = 1260$ passwords

    b. There would be 36 more choices for the second character, or $36 \times 1 = 36$ more passwords.

2. $(12 \times 11) \div 2 = 66$ topping combinations (assuming order is irrelevant)

3. **a.** $36^4 + 36^5 + 36^6 = 2{,}238{,}928{,}128$ passwords

    b. $2{,}238{,}928{,}128 \div 10^6 \approx 2239$ seconds, or approximately 37.3 minutes

4. **a.** $10^4 = 10{,}000$ PINs

    b. Since $\frac{76{,}500}{10{,}000} = 7.65$, we would expect each PIN to be used, on the average, by 7 or 8 customers.

counting tree   A diagram that shows all the possible ways a set of choices—each with one or more options—can be made. The counting tree below shows the possible three-number lock sequences for a push-button lock with three buttons—labeled 1, 2, and 3—if repeated numbers are not allowed.

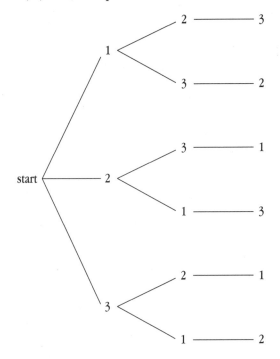

network   A collection of points, or nodes, connected by edges. A network is also called a *graph*. The first network has two nodes and three edges. The second network has four nodes and five edges. In this unit, students find the number of paths through a network. In the second network shown below, for example, there are four paths from node A to node D.

Index

Index